9/90

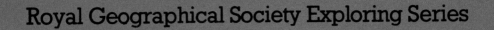

Royal Geographical Society Exploring Series

EXPLORING THE HIMALAYAS

Ian Cameron

Longman

Contents

Royal Geographical Society

Exploring the Himalayas has been written with the help of the Royal Geographical Society. This Society has been working for more than 150 years "for the promotion of that most important and entertaining branch of knowledge, geography." In the past it sponsored many of the world's great explorers – Livingstone in Africa, Scott and Shackleton in the Antarctic, Hillary and Tenzing on Everest. Today it is busier than ever. It has the world's largest private collection of maps, and a magnificent library; its publications and lectures play a leading role in geographical teaching and research; more than 100 expeditions apply to it annually for help, and each year it sends large numbers of explorers, research-workers, scientists and conservationists to the farthest ends of the Earth.

I should like to thank the Royal Geographical Society very much indeed for their support and encouragement, for allowing me the use of their library, map-room and archives, and for providing most of the book's illustrations.

Ian Cameron

Cover: Climbers on their way to Kangchenjunga in the eastern Himalayas.

Back cover: Heavily laden porters at the approaches to Everest.

Endpapers: Kongur, one of the great peaks in the Chinese Pamir.

Title page: An expedition camped in a valley south of Everest. "Here is some of the most beautiful scenery on Earth."

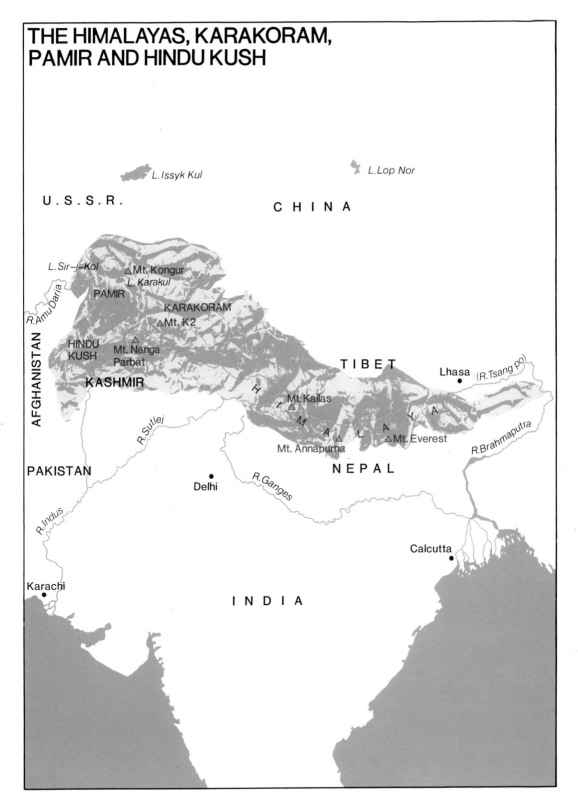

THE HIMALAYAS, KARAKORAM, PAMIR AND HINDU KUSH

L.Issyk Kul

L.Lop Nor

U.S.S.R.

C H I N A

L.Sir-i-Kol

△Mt.Kongur
L.Karakul

PAMIR

KARAKORAM

△Mt. K2

R.Amu Daria

HINDU
KUSH

△
Mt. Nanga
Parbat

KASHMIR

AFGHANISTAN

T I B E T

Lhasa
(R.Tsang po)

H
I
M
A
L
A
Y
A

△Mt. Kailas

R.Sutlej

△
Mt. Annapurna

△Mt. Everest

R.Brahmaputra

PAKISTAN

Delhi

R.Ganges

N E P A L

R.Indus

Calcutta

Karachi

I N D I A

The Roof of the World

Because Himalaya is a Sanskrit word, the correct pronunciation is for the emphasis to be on the first and not the second 'a', this 'a' being long, as in 'car'. Academically, the plural of Himalaya is Himalaya and *not* Himalayas. However, the Anglicized form Himalayas has been used so widely and for so long that I have kept to it throughout.

*   *   *

Approx. area: 418,500 square kilometres (Himalayas, Karakoram, Pamir and Hindu Kush)
Highest point: 8,848 metres (Mount Everest)
Highest annual rainfall: 1,077 centimetres (Cherapungi, Meghalaya)
Lowest annual rainfall: 1.25 centimetres (Lake Karakul, Pamir)
Highest recorded temperature: probably 49·8°C (upper Indus valley)
Lowest recorded temperature: probably −47·0°C (north face of Everest).

The name Himalaya comes from two ancient Sanskrit words, *hima*, meaning snow, and *alaya* meaning home. It was the mountains of Nepal which were first called the "Home of Snow". Gradually this name became extended to the mountains that border Nepal, until today it is used for the whole great range which stretches for more than 2,400 kilometres from the River Indus in the west to the River Brahmaputra in the east.

The Himalayas, together with their neighbouring ranges the Karakoram, Pamir and Hindu Kush, are the highest and the most magnificent mountains on Earth. Yet they are also very nearly the youngest mountains on Earth. Four million years ago, at a time when great ranges like the Urals and the Rockies were already old, they didn't exist. In the place where they stand today was a deep sea. How you may wonder, were the highest mountains on Earth raised up out of one of the deepest seas?

According to Hindu legend a pair of seagulls used to live on the shore of a deep ocean. Each year the female gull laid her eggs some way inland; but each year the sea swept in and washed the eggs away. Eventually the gulls cried out to Vishnu, the Preserver of Life, to help them. Vishnu heard the seagulls' cry and took pity on them. He opened his mouth and swallowed the sea. Looking down, he saw be-

"The north-facing slopes of the Himalayas are totally different from the south-facing slopes." Above: the bleak Donkia Pass looking into Tibet, painted by the 19th century naturalist Joseph Hooker. Below: Dal Lake in the fertile Vale of Kashmir, painted by the 19th century soldier Major Molyneux.

neath him, in the place where the sea had been, the newly-created Mother Earth. Content – and maybe exhausted after so much drinking! – Vishnu fell asleep. But as he slept, the demon Hiranyanksha leapt on Mother Earth and raped her: raped her with such brutal violence that her bones were broken and levered up, high into the clouds, thus forming the Himalayas.

That is one explanation of how the mountains were formed. Scientists give us another explanation.

About 90 million years ago, the scientists say, the Earth consisted of two super-continents: Laurasia in the north and Gondwana in the south, with a deep sea lying between them. Gondwana gradually broke up into five separate landmasses: South America, Africa, Australia, Antarctica and India. These land-masses, with one exception, then drifted slowly into the positions they occupy today. The exception was India, which moved much farther and much faster than its neighbours. India, in fact, drifted right out of the southern hemisphere and into the northern. On its way it passed over one of the hot spots in the surface of the Earth, and so became encrusted with a great mass of molten lava. Then, like a gigantic battering-ram, it crashed into the underbelly of Asia. The underbelly of Asia consisted of soft, sedimentary rocks; and it was these rocks which, as the continents collided, were

squeezed up, like toothpaste between the closing walls of a vice, to form the Himalayas and their associated ranges.

Since these ranges – the Himalayas, the Karakoram, the Pamir and the Hindu Kush – were all formed in the same way and at the same time, one would expect them to have a lot in common. And they do. One thing they have in common is that they are still in the process of being created. For the battering-ram of India is *still* boring into the underbelly of Asia, and the great peaks are *still* being thrust up, in some places by as much as 10 or 12 centimetres a year – hence the old joke that someone had better climb Everest quickly before it got too high! Perhaps the most obvious thing the ranges have in common is their sheer size. If you transferred just one of them – the Himalayas – on to the map of Europe, it would stretch from the English Channel to the Black Sea. And not only are the ranges big in size, things happen in them in a big way. Avalanches rip away whole mountainsides; floods devastate whole valleys; for as Joseph Hooker (a 19th century botanist) put it, "upon what a gigantic scale does Nature here operate!" Another thing the ranges have in common is that their north-facing slopes are totally different from their south-facing slopes. The reason for this is the weather. Millions of years ago the south-east monsoon used to bring rain each summer to the whole of central Asia. Central Asia in those days was covered with thick forests and fertile plains. Then, as the mountains started to rise, the troubles of central Asia began. For as the mountains rose, so the monsoon rain-clouds had to rise also. This forced the clouds to drop their rain prematurely. The higher the mountains rose, the fewer clouds got over them. The rainfall of central Asia became less and less, until the thick forests and fertile plains were transformed to arid wastes of sand. Today the contrast between the south-face of the mountains and the north-face is sudden and dramatic. In the south the mountain-slopes are thickly populated, and covered with great forests and the most beautiful carpets of flowers. In the north the mountain-slopes are sparsely populated, and covered with bare scree and dessicated rock. The illustrations on pages 8 and 9 show us this difference more eloquently than words.

Since the country to the north of the mountains is so very different from the country to the south, it is not surprising that the people are different too.

North of the mountains, the people are Mongoloids. The Mongoloids are a short, thickset, olive-skinned people, with little hair on their bodies; they have flattish faces and slit eyes, their eyes being deep-set to protect them from wind and snow-glare. Since the land they live in is barren, they have been obliged to become nomads, driving their sheep, yaks, goats, camels and horses vast distances from one sparse pasture to the next. They build no cities, but live in big round portable tents called *yurts*. The Mongoloids are a proud, hospitable but warlike people. Their kingdom, it has been said, is the back of a horse; and it was their horsemen who formed the much-feared armies of Genghis Khan and Tamerlane.

South of the mountains the people are a mixture of Negroid and Caucasoid. The Negroid/Caucasoids are a slim, small-boned and graceful people; they often have curly hair and almond-shaped eyes. Because the land they live in is fertile, they have become farmers, living in villages. And because the south face of the mountains is split up into a number of steep-sided valleys, the Negroid/Caucasoids have split up into a number of small self-contained ethnic divisions, each working out its own particular way of life to suit its own particular valley. (There are nineteen of these different ethnic divisions in Nepal alone.) The Negroid/Caucasoids are a disunited but relatively peaceful people; they lead static lives, many of them never venturing out of the valley in which they were born.

The Himalayas and their adjoining ranges have, from time immemorial, acted as a barrier which has divided the warlike Mongoloids of the north from the peaceful Negroids and Caucasoids of the south. This barrier, however, has never been watertight. There has always been a safety valve. What happened was this. As the climate of central Asia got worse and the land became increasingly arid, so the people who lived there found themselves facing increasingly difficult conditions. In search of the richer pastures which they knew existed in the south, they migrated in little groups through the mountain passes. (A good example are the Sherpas. Six hundred years ago the Sherpas lived well to the north of Everest. Today they live well to the south.) So for thousands of years the Mongoloids have been slowly but persistently filtering through the mountains.

The story of the Himalayas, Karakoram, Pamir and Hindu Kush needs to be seen against this background: a background in which the Mongoloids have been trying always to push south, and the Negroid/Caucasoids have been trying always to keep them back. It would have been nice to be able to say that the story of the mountains has been an uncomplicated struggle between man and nature, with explorers and climbers pitting their skills against the most formidable peaks on Earth. But the truth isn't so simple. Almost every other climber in the Himalayas and the Hindu Kush has been a soldier or a political agent; almost every other explorer has been a spy. There have been very nearly as many columns of troops pushing into the mountains, as there have been expeditions. The exploration of the Himalayas has been very much dependent on strategy and politics.

The contrasting types of Himalayan people.
Above: Mongoloids from Lhasa.
Below: Negroid/Caucasians from Kathmandu;
Painted at the turn of the century by Henry Oldfield.

1 Invaders through the Snow

It used to be thought that most of the world was discovered by European seamen and travellers between the 16th and 19th centuries. This view, however, is now recognised as erroneous; for a lot of the so-called "discoveries" by Europeans were re-discoveries. The people of the ancient world were great travellers, and many of the Earth's remote mountain-peaks and river-sources were known to the ancients long before their "discovery" was claimed by people from Europe.

The Himalayas are a case in point. The first people to explore them were almost certainly Hindu pilgrims, who climbed the peaks and followed the rivers to their sources more than a thousand years before the birth of Christ.

The Hindus loved the Himalayas; for the great mountains brought them water, and the water brought them life. They built shrines on the mountain-tracks. They set-up prayer flags on the mountain-slopes. They plunged into the mountain-snows with the same ecstasy as they plunged into the sacred waters of the Ganges. They worshipped the peaks as gods. And there was one peak which the Hindus regarded as particularly sacred. This was Mount Kailas. *"Mount Kailas"*, according to the book of Hindu legends the *Mahabharata*, *"is the monarch of all mountains: a never-tiring worker for the common good. Its slopes are covered with forests. Its rivers are covered with golden lotus. Near its summit is the hall of Brahma: a hall full of fountains, out of which there flows for ever the elixir of life."* Why, one wonders, should Mount Kailas have been singled out for such particular praise?

If you visit Kailas today you will find it a beautiful but comparatively minor mountain on the rim of the Tibetan plateau, far to the north of the main ranges of the Himalayas. It is remote and barren. There isn't a forest in sight, much less a golden lotus or a fountain! So one

Mount Kailas: the Hindus' holy mountain, source of the four great rivers of India.

Alexander the Great, the first European to campaign in the Hindu Kush and the Pamir.

wonders even more: why did the Hindus consider it so holy? There can be only one answer. The Hindus worshipped Kailas because they recognised the mountain as the watershed from which stem the life-bringing rivers of almost the whole of northern India. For it is here, within a few kilometres of Kailas, that the four great rivers of India – the Indus, Sutlej, Brahmaputra and Ganges – all have their source. The Hindus were therefore right, symbolically, to describe Kailas as "full of fountains". And the point is this: to acquire such knowledge Hindu pilgrims must have crossed the Himalayas, skirted the Karakoram, penetrated deep into the Tibetan plateau and traced the Indus, Sutlej, Brahmaputra and Ganges to their sources. These were great feats of exploration, carried out long before people from Europe ever set foot in the mountains.

The first people from Europe who *did* set foot in the mountains were almost certainly the troops of Alexander the Great. Alexander's troops may never have seen the main ranges of the Himalayas; but they crossed the Hindu Kush, and they campaigned and climbed in the Pamir.

It was in the winter of 329 B.C. that Alexander attempted to cross the Hindu Kush. Two things make us realise how impossible a task this must have seemed. Alexander's enemies were so convinced a crossing was impossible that they never even bothered to guard the passes; and no army was to attempt a similar crossing for more than 1,500 years. Alexander's route was *via* the Khaiwak Pass in Afghanistan. And what a nightmare crossing it must have been! The pass was deep in snow. It was bitterly cold. The soldiers had little food, and no wood with which to make fires. As they floundered through waist-high snow-drifts, they suffered terribly from frostbite and exhaustion. The rarified air made it difficult for them to breathe. Men and horses died in their thousands, many of them frozen solid to the rocks as they leaned against them. Alexander lost more men and more animals crossing the Hindu Kush than in all his campaigns in central Asia. But his troops got through; and from that day to this the

13

passes of the Hindu Kush have been recognised as a potential invasion-route between the plains of India and the plains of central Asia.

Next year Alexander led his army into the Pamir, and here again his exploits were remarkable. His enemies, the Sogdians, fled to the Koh-i-nor, a natural fortress, its great walls of rock rising sheer for about three kilometres into the sky. When Alexander called on the Sogdians to surrender, they laughed and told him to go and find troops with wings. However, it was Alexander who had the last laugh. He called for volunteer-mountaineers from among his troops, offering them the equivalent of two years' pay if they reached the summit. Three-hundred would-be climbers came forward. They were given flax-ropes and iron tent-pegs; and that night by the pale light of the stars, they moved into position at the bottom of a rock-face which looked so unclimbable that it wasn't guarded. But Alexander's troops climbed it. Every few metres they hammered their tent-pegs into crevices in the rock, lassooed them, and hauled themselves up on the end of their ropes. Thirty fell to their death. But as the first streaks of dawn appeared in the sky, the survivors stood triumphant on the summit. When the Sogdians saw them, they thought they must be more than mortal, and surrendered.

Alexander proved that the mountains *could* be crossed, and *could* be climbed; but only at a cost.

More than fifteen hundred years were to pass before the mountains again echoed to the tramp of such large numbers of troops. And the troops of this next invading army were not foot-soldiers but cavalry: the much feared Mongol horsemen of the Golden Horde. In 1219 Genghis Khan led his Golden Horde of 200,000 cavalry westward over the Steppes, sacking one after another the prosperous centres of the Muslim world which lay on the north-facing slopes of the mountains. Each time Genghis Khan sacked a city, he caused the most terrible devastation and suffering. He massacred everything and everybody: men, women, children, even the animals. *"The horsemen came,"* wrote an eyewitness, *"they*

"Likeness of His Majesty the Amir Timur (Tamerlane). Lord of the happy conjunction, King of the throne". A contemporary portrait.

uprooted, they burned, they slew, they despoiled, they departed . . . Our splendours are wiped off the Earth as writing is wiped off paper. Our palaces have become the home of the owl and the raven." For centuries the cities which lay to the north of the mountains had been struggling against a worsening climate and a shortage of water. Being sacked by the Mongols was for some of them the last straw. They never recovered.

In the rich towns of India people heard of the terrible things that were happening in the north. They looked at the Himalayas and the Hindu Kush, and gave thanks to their gods that the mountains were there to protect them, "a shield against the Barbarians". But the Hindu Kush, as Alexander had proved, was a shield that *could* be pierced; and in the 14th century it was pierced by Tamerlane.

Tamerlane was a plunderer – probably the most brutal the world has ever known. Of all his plunderings, that of India was the cruellest. It left a legacy of terror, which, from that day to this, has had an influence on the way people have felt about the Himalayas and Hindu Kush. Tamerlane made no bones about his motives for invading India. *"I came to Hindustan,"* he wrote, *"to lead a campaign to the death against the infidel, to convert them to the true faith, to purify their land from the abomination of idolatry, to overthrow their temples, and to seize their riches, since plunder taken in war is as lawful to our people as mother's milk."* In March 1398 he led his army into the Hindu Kush. His army consisted of roughly 90,000 men, and about the same number of horses and pack-mules. They established a camp on the north-facing slopes of the mountains, and Tamerlane sent an advance-guard to pioneer a route and clear it of opposition. The opposition to his crossing came from the Nuristani, an isolated race of mountain-people, who, rumour had it, were black as night, tall as giants, eaters of fire, and so fierce that they had never been conquered. They proved no match, however, for the Mongol archers, who stormed their mountain-strongholds with disciplined ferocity. The Nuristani women and children were carried off as slaves. The Nuristani men were massacred, and their skulls piled into victory cones, "so high they pierced the very clouds". Tamerlane's army then moved up to the pass which had been used fifteen hundred years earlier by Alexander: the Khaiwak. Like Alexander before him, Tamerlane suffered heavy casualties crossing the Khaiwak Pass. His men had to force their way through deep drifts of snow. His animals became bogged down, and had to be dragged along, a few metres at a time, on wooden sledges. In some places the whole army had to be lowered by ropes down the face of enormous cliffs. In other places rope bridges had to be suspended over the ravines, and men and animals swung precariously across. Something

like 20,000 of Tamerlane's troops are believed to have died of cold, exposure and exhaustion during the crossing. But by September the survivors stood on the banks of the Sutlej. The rich cities of the Indian plain lay before them, ripe for plunder.

What took place next was not a battle. It was a holocaust. Each time Tamerlane defeated a Hindu army or captured a Hindu town, the same pattern was repeated. If the Hindus resisted, they were massacred. If they surrendered they were still massacred. As Tamerlane advanced on Delhi he left in his wake a trail of burnt crops, razed cities and something like a million dead. By December his army was camped on the plains outside the Hindu capital.

The battle that followed was one of the bloodiest in history. As a prelude, Tamerlane ordered that all the prisoners he had taken should be put to death. *"It was done within the hour. 50,000, more or less. Some say 100,000. God alone knows the exact number."* Next day the armies met on the plains of Jumna. The Hindus had great expectations of their elephants. Tamerlane, however, scattered spikes of iron in places where he thought the elephants would charge. These got entangled in the great creatures' feet, and brought them to a halt. *"Then Tamerlane ordered 500 swift camels to be laden with reeds soaked in oil. The reeds were set on fire, so that the camels cried out and rushed at the elephants. Whereat the elephants, who feared both camels and fire, turned in terror and mutilated their drivers and trod them underfoot, and trampled down great numbers of their own infantry. So the Army of Hind got no use from their elephants . . . All day the battle raged, until the Army of Darkness was put to flight and the way to Delha* (Delhi) *lay open."*

You can guess what happened next. Delhi surrendered; and in the hope of saving lives, an enormous ransom was handed over. The Mongol troops, however, got out of hand, and having collected the ransom, they set fire to the city and massacred the entire population. *"It was clearly the will of God,"* wrote Tamerlane, *"that this disaster should befall so evil a city."* After the annihilation of the Indian army,

15

Zao Pass, N.W Frontier

A typical pass in the Hindu Kush, painted by Colonel Holdich.

the rich towns of the plains were systematically looted and their inhabitants killed. Places associated with the Hindu faith were singled out for particularly brutal treatment: *"On the banks of this abominable river* (the Ganges) *every man, woman, child and living creature was despatched to the fires of hell."* At the end of six months' plundering, Tamerlane needed an additional 10,000 pack-mules to carry his loot. It was time, he decided, to head for home. So, laying waste the rich farmland to the south of the Himalayas, the Mongols retraced their steps. One moment they were looting and massacring; next moment they had disappeared into the Afghan valleys as suddenly as they had emerged.

They left behind them a world in ruins: crops burned, irrigation-systems shattered, towns reduced to rubble and ash, upward of 5 million dead, and a legacy of chaos, famine and disease from which it took the people of India hundreds of years to recover.

The Mongol invasion has never been forgotten in India. From that day to this the people of the sub-continent have looked at the Himalayas and the Hindu Kush and wondered just how effective a barrier their mountains are. This has affected their whole attitude to the mountains. They have been almost obsessively concerned with the passes that run through them. For they have been very much afraid that what had happened once might happen again.

2 The Search for the Forbidden City

In the undiscovered regions of the world there has often been a particular goal which explorers have longed to reach. In the Sahara many explorers' goal was Timbuktu; in Antarctica it was the South Pole; in the Himalayas it was the forbidden city of Lhasa.

"The Forbidden City" was the name given by Europeans to both Peking, the capital of China, and Lhasa, the capital of Tibet. To those who lived in Europe, Peking and Lhasa were almost equally remote and mysterious. Both cities were thought to be full of bizarre and fabulous treasures; both were known to be fiercely guarded and taboo to foreigners. However, of the two forbidden cities it was Lhasa which was the more difficult for Europeans to get to. For whereas the capital of China lay in a fertile and thickly-populated plain, the capital of Tibet lay in a high and sparsely-populated plateau ringed by snow-covered mountains. No wonder Lhasa became the most sought after goal of travellers from the West.

We can be fairly certain who was the first European to set foot in Lhasa. In 1245 the Franciscan Friar John of Carpine visited Mongolia, and talked to people who *came* from Lhasa. In 1254 another Friar, William of Rubruck, visited Sinkiang and penetrated some way onto the Tibetan plateau in the direction of Lhasa. In 1272, in an epic journey of exploration, Marco Polo crossed the Pamir and the Takla Makan desert, and cut across the corner of Tibet. There is no evidence, however, that any of these early travellers got as far as Lhasa.

The first European who we know definitely visited the "Forbidden City" is the Jesuit priest Johann Grueber. Jesuit priests were among the first people from Europe to set eyes on the oases of the Sahara, the headwaters of the Mississippi, the peaks of the Andes and the beaches of Japan. It shouldn't therefore surprise us that they were among the first Europeans to explore the Himalayas. What *is* perhaps surprising is the direction they came from. For Grueber and his travelling-companion D'Orville approached Lhasa not from the south but from the north: not *via* India but *via* China.

There was, in the 17th century, a Jesuit mission in Peking; and it seems that Grueber was sent to this mission with a definite task in mind, that of trying to find a trade route between China and the West *via* India. Grueber spent three years in Peking preparing for his journey. He learned several central Asian languages and became a first-class surveyor. On 13th April, 1661 together with the Belgian Father Albert D'Orville, he left Peking, well provided with passports and surveying gear. It took the two priests a couple of months to reach Sining-fu, a city which had grown up around one of the gates in the Great Wall of China. Grueber describes this Great Wall as *"very high, and so broad that Six Horsemen may ride abreast on it without embarrassing each other."* Leaving the wall behind them, the Fathers headed southwest into the desert. And the unknown.

To start with their route lay over the Takla Makan. *"Now"* (we are told) *"they entered a vast and barren waste of sand, which, some say, stretches from India to the Great Frozen Ocean of the North. This waste of sand is inhabited by Tartars who rove up and down it to rob Caravans, and at certain Seasons settle with their portable Cities* (i.e. tents) *along the banks of the few small rivers. This is the desert which Marco Polo said was haunted by Spirits. But Grueber makes no mention of them."* The Fathers must have been thankful to come, in midsummer, to Lake Koko Nor near the northern border of Tibet. Skirting this lake, they pushed on to the bleak Tibetan plateau. How one wishes that Grueber had left us a description of this plateau! But, alas, to quote a former president of the Royal Geographical Society, "the Father was not very communicative". Grueber seems to have been more interested in surveying than in scenery, more

The Potala in Lhasa, the Tibetans' holy palace-monastery-fortress: a drawing by the Jesuit priest Johann Grueber who, in 1661, was the first European to enter Lhasa.

at home with religious dogma than with people. All he tells us of the Tibetan plateau is that it was barren, and that in crossing it he and D'Orville "suffered much". We must therefore conjure up our own picture of the two priests as they struggled antlike, week after week, across the roof of the world: tiny figures, dwarfed by an immensity of rock and sky. It was a land of salt-pan, scree and bitter wind through which they travelled: a land where even the deepest valleys were 3,350 metres above sea-level and almost devoid of trees or grass. No wonder they suffered. Eventually they came to the Kun Lun Mountains, which they crossed by a 4,570 metres pass waist-deep in snow. They were only just in time; for it was autumn, and in another couple of weeks the mountains would have been impassable. They sighted Lhasa on October 7th, and entered the city next morning.

Again, how one wishes that Grueber had given us a description of Lhasa. Here he was, the first European to set eyes on "the For-

bidden City"; and 99% of his Diary consists of a dull analysis of Tibetan politics and a learned comparison of the Buddhist and Catholic faiths. The latter, it must be said, ends with a most interesting observation. *"It is amazing* (Grueber writes) *how the Buddhist religion agrees with the Romish. For Buddhists too celebrate Mass with bread and wine; they too give extreme unction, bless those who are married, say prayers for the sick, form processions, sing in choirs, honour the relics of idols, build monasteries and nunneries, observe fasts, undergo penances, consecrate holy men, and send out missionaries who travel vast distances barefoot and live in poverty."* He might also have added that both faiths have the story of an immaculate conception (or virgin birth). Grueber was a man of great intelligence. His intelligence, however, was directed towards things spiritual, not temporal. He showed little interest in recording the everyday life of the Tibetan people. He did, however, make several excellent sketches of the Potala, a building which he nicely describes as *"a Castle built upon a high Mountain, after the European Fashion, wherein the Lama holds a numerous Court"*. Also he was the first European to describe accurately the much-used Tibetan prayer-wheel, and the much-used Tibetan greeting associated with it – *"Om mane padme hum"* (Hail, oh jewel in the lotus) which is the Tibetan equivalent of our "Hullo" and "Good-bye". While his description of Tibetan hair-styles helps prove the saying that there is nothing new under the sun. *"The ladies braid or Curl their Hair* (he wrote) *in the manner of Laces or small bonds. On their Foreheads they wear a red bandeau, and on the top of their heads they have a ridge of hair bedecked with Turchoises and Corals."*

Grueber and D'Orville spent six weeks in Lhasa. Then they set out to try and do what no European had ever done before – and few since – to cut through the very heart of the Himalayas from north to south. Surprisingly, they made the attempt in winter. And, even more surprisingly, they succeeded.

Leaving Lhasa the two Fathers headed south-west. After four days they came to the main range of the Himalayas, and found themselves staring up at the north face of the Cho-Oyu/Everest massif, the highest and most awesome mountain-complex on Earth. There is only one pass across this formidable massif, the Thung La, a windlashed gap between peaks whose height Grueber correctly calculated at over 5,500 metres. "At this altitude," the priest remarks laconically, "the air is so rarified we found it almost impossible to breathe." It was November, and the snow was several metres deep. Somehow, Grueber and D'Orville struggled over the Thung La, a feat of which experienced Alpinists would have been proud. They then found themselves in the gorge of the Bhotia-Kosi River. They had skirted Everest, and were probably the first Europeans to sight its summit.

Grueber and D'Orville were now surrounded by spectacular scenery. In the course of the next few weeks they must have swung over some of the most hazardous bridges on Earth, edged their way along some of the most perilous paths on Earth, and gazed at some of the most beautiful mountains on Earth. Yet Grueber makes no mention of the majestic peaks which soared up all around them. This may surprise as well as disappoint us. However, the fact is that before the Romantic movement of the late 18th century, hardly anyone appreciated the beauties of the natural world. Mountains in Grueber's day were regarded not as beautiful, but as ugly – "a Universe of death which God by curse created Evil". It would have been surprising if Grueber *had* waxed eloquent over the wonders of the Bhotia-Kosi. We must therefore rely on the account of a later explorer, the Pundit Hari Ram, to give us an idea of what the gorge must have been like. *"The river ran through a gigantic chasm* (the Pundit writes) *many thousands of feet deep, but so narrow it was spanned by a bridge of only 24 paces. Near this bridge the precipices were so sheer, the path had to be supported on iron pegs let into the face of the rock. This path was formed by bars of iron and slabs of stone stretching from peg to peg and covered with earth. It is nowhere more than 18 inches* (45 centimetres) *in width, and often no more than 9 inches* (23 centimetres). *It continues for more than a third of a mile* (two fifths of a kilometre) *some 1,500 feet* (450 metres) *above the river which can be seen roaring below in its narrow bed."* The Fathers did well to cover the 400 odd kilometres between Lhasa, the capital of Tibet, and Kathmandu, the capital of Nepal, in less than three weeks.

Grueber was not impressed with the Nepalese. *"They daub themselves,"* he wrote, *"with a nasty kind of oil, which causes them to stink intolerably . . . also they have a most cruel Custom: when they judge sick people to be past hope of Recovery, they carry them into the Fields and casting them into deep ditches leave them to perish, and their bodies to be Devoured by Birds of Prey."* The Fathers hurried on to Agra (near Delhi), which they reached almost exactly a year after setting out from

Peking. Here the patient and self-effacing Albert D'Orville died. "The hardships he had endured," we are told, "had altogether drained his strength." Grueber continued his journey alone, arriving at the Vatican in Rome in June, 1663.

This was a fine piece of exploration, and it is surprising that Grueber and D'Orville are not better known. Perhaps their obscurity is due partly to their unwordly characters, and partly to the fact that the route they pioneered was far too difficult to be used for trade. There is, however, no denying the fact that several explorers who are household names made less remarkable journeys than these tough but "not very communicative" priests.

*   *   *

Grueber's and D'Orville's visit to Lhasa did little to lift the veil of mystery that surrounded the city; for Grueber's Diary was never published, and few people knew that his journey had taken place. It was the same story with the next European to visit Lhasa, Ippolito Desideri. Desideri was also a Jesuit priest. His visit lasted longer than Grueber's. He spent nearly five years in and around Lhasa – from 1716 to 1721 – first setting up a mission, then watching the Mongols invade Tibet and the Chinese drive the Mongols out. His Diary contains a lot of fascinating – and horrifying – material. It was not, however, published until the 20th century; so his visit, too, did little to make Lhasa better known in the West. The first Englishman to reach Lhasa, Thomas Manning, entered the city in 1811. Manning managed to get through to Lhasa whereas abler explorers failed, partly because he was a doctor, and partly because he grovelled unashamedly to the Chinese. *"I was always seeking,"* he wrote, *"to kertse* (curtsey) *kow-tow* (bow) *or kneel; and if there was an option between making one kertse or three, I invariably chose to make three."* Unfortunately for Manning, when he arrived back in India his account of his travels was not believed; so his Diary, too, never saw the light of day. It was as though events were conspiring to keep the "Forbidden City" veiled in mystery. This impression was heightened by

the experiences of the next two travellers who reached the Tibetan capital. In 1846 the French priests, Evarist Huc and Joseph Gabet, spent two months in Lhasa, and a further four months exploring the Tibetan plateau. Huc wrote a splendid and highly entertaining account of their travels. However, his account turned out to be a bit *too* entertaining; for his racey style and his habit of recounting Tibetan legend as though it was fact, were frowned on by traditional scholars. His story was dismissed as "frivolous"; it, too, was discredited. The result was that right up to the beginning of the 20th century Lhasa remained veiled in mystery. This veil, however, was then ripped violently aside. For the next Westerners to set foot in the forbidden city carried with them not the cross of Christ, but the flag of empire.

*   *   *

It was the British who, in 1904, invaded Tibet and occupied the "Forbidden City": an unhappy event summed up by Peter Fleming in his book *Bayonets to Lhasa: "Its outward aspect was swashbuckling, its inner history ambiguous, its aftermath unedifying. Over it there hangs, as over some indiscretion, an air of apology and embarrassment."*

The architect of the invasion was Lord Curzon, the Viceroy of India. Curzon was afraid that Tibet was about to be swallowed up, like so much of central Asia, by the ever-expanding empire of Russia. He therefore offered the Tibetans a treaty of friendship, to guarantee their neutrality. So far so good. What wasn't so good was that when the Tibetans showed signs of declining the proposed treaty, Curzon decided to send a "diplomatic mission" to Lhasa, to force the Dalai Lama to toe the British line. This "diplomatic mission" consisted of eleven hundred troops and nearly eleven thousand baggage-carriers! Its military commander was Brigadier-General Macdonald. Its real leader was Francis Younghusband.

Some historians would have us believe that Younghusband was "a firebrand, a thruster". This, however, is too simple a judgement. It is true that Younghusband was a doer, a man who was always eager (to use his own words) to "get a move on". But he was also a mystic, who set great store by spiritual values; he was the founder of the Congress of Faiths, an organisation devoted to breaking down the barriers between the world's religions. Younghusband in fact had a lot in common with Gordon of Khartoum; and if at the approaches to Lhasa it had been Younghusband who was massacred by the Tibetans instead of the other way round, the "firebrand" might well have acquired the same saintly image as Gordon.

In the autumn of 1903 Curzon ordered Younghusband to join an expeditionary force of British officers and Sikh and Gurkha troops who were camped on the Tibetan border. Younghusband's Diary tells us what happened next. *"As I looked out of my tent each morning I enjoyed what is perhaps the most beautiful panorama in all the world: the unbroken chain of the Himalaya, shining out in dazzling whiteness . . . On December 6th, after months of arguing with a people very nearly as obstinate as ourselves, we realized that our political objective would not be attained until we ad-*

Right: Francis Younghusband. Below: the wall across the Chumbi Valley which Younghusband had to pass through in order to enter Tibet.

vanced into the country. A move was therefore ordered, and a considerable body of troops crossed over the Jelap La Pass and into the Chumbi valley."

In the Chumbi valley the Tibetans had built a wall across the one and only road; and the wall was defended. Younghusband arranged a meeting with the Tibetan general who was in charge of the wall. At the meeting, Younghusband explained his reasons for entering Tibet, and made a solemn promise never to attack the Tibetans unless they attacked him first. *"Next morning,"* Younghusband wrote, *"as we came out of the pine forest where we had camped for the night, we could see the wall built right across the road and high up the*

mountainside on either hand. Whether we should have to fight our way through, or whether the general would respond to my arguments, had yet to be proved, and Macdonald took every military precaution. But to our enormous relief we saw that the door in the wall was open, and we were soon passing peacably through."

The troops spent three weeks in the Chumbi valley; then they were on the move again. *"On January 8th, in the very depths of winter, we crossed the Tang-la Pass and advanced onto the Tibetan plateau. I shall never forget that day. Reveille sounded at dawn, and as I looked out of my tent the very spirit of Frost seemed to have settled on the scene. The stars were shooting out sharp rays into a steely sky. Behind the great peak of Chumalhari the first beams of dawn were showing, but with no force yet to cheer or warm, and only sufficient light to make the cold more apparent. The poor Sikhs were crawling out of their tents so shrivelled with cold it looked as though if they shrivelled any more, there would be nothing left of them."*

The army advanced on to the plateau as far as Tuna, a village of no significance in the middle of nowhere. Macdonald didn't like the look of Tuna, and retreated to the Chumbi valley, leaving Younghusband with a skeleton force to see through the winter. Winter turned out to be a time of endless blizzard and fruitless negotiation. *"Every morning,"* Younghusband wrote, *"a terrific wind would arise and blow with fury for the rest of the day. Mighty masses of cloud would come sweeping up from India, snow would fall, the mountains would be hidden, and our camp would be the very picture of desolation. It seemed impossible that the poor sentries at night could stand against the howling storm and the penetrating snow, let alone resist an attack by the Tibetans."* In the brief spells of fine weather Younghusband did everything he could to bring about a negotiated settlement. But the Tibetans didn't want to negotiate; they wanted the British to leave. Eventually Younghusband rode, alone and unarmed, into the Tibetan army's camp: a move of great courage but doubtful wisdom. He was well received by the

officers, but not so well received by the lamas. It was in fact the lamas who turned out to be the stumbling-block to a settlement. They insisted that their religion required them to ban all foreigners from their country. Younghusband was not impressed. He felt that the lamas were afraid of foreigners not because they saw them as a threat to their religion, but because they saw them as a threat to their priestly privileges. He was probably right. Most Tibetan lamas entered a monastery not through spiritual vocation, but through economic necessity; and they were the high priests not only of Tibet's religion, but also of Tibet's feudal system – a system rigidly opposed to any sort of change. So the lamas now accused Younghusband of being no more than a common bandit, and tried to persuade the army officers to kill him. It was as Younghusband put it "a damned ticklish situation"; but by pretending the whole affair was a joke he managed to bluff his way out of trouble and back to Tuna.

In the spring Younghusband and Macdonald again advanced on Lhasa. Soon, at a place called Guru, they came face to face with the Tibetan army entrenched behind a barricade. This was the moment of truth.

For the better part of a day the two armies stood facing one another: a little over 1,000 British troops, a little under 3,000 Tibetan troops. There was a meeting, but it came to nothing. Again and again Macdonald begged Younghusband to let him attack. And again and again Younghusband refused. He was determined, no matter what the cost, to keep his promise, and not be the first to shed blood. Eventually the British column, under an ash-grey sky, advanced in close formation towards the barricade without firing a shot. These were quixotic, indeed suicidal, tactics. For the British troops had to walk slowly up to a wall from behind which something like a thousand rifles were trained on them at point-blank range. If the Tibetans had opened fire, the

Right: photographs taken by Younghusband's expedition. Above: Tibetan bodies after the massacre at Guru; "It was" wrote Younghusband, "a terrible and ghastly business". Below: Troops marching into the Forbidden City.

Mysteries of the Buddhist faith encountered by the expedition. Left: Buddhist monks. Right: a Buddhist altar.

British would have been decimated. But the Tibetans didn't fire; and the British troops walked round the end of the barricade, and took up position in the Tibetans' rear. The road to Lhasa lay open. It looked as though Younghusband had won a famous and bloodless victory.

Then things began to go wrong. The British made the mistake of trying to disarm the Tibetans. This may have made sense in military terms, but not in human terms. No troops like laying down their arms, and the Tibetans were particularly reluctant to do this, because their rifles were often their own property, and their swords were often family heirlooms. As the Sikhs and Gurkhas tried to take away the Tibetans' weapons, there were angry scuffles. One of the Tibetan generals rode his horse into the mêlée. A Sikh grabbed his bridle. And the general, at point blank range, shot away half the Sikh's face.

There was a moment of shocked silence. Then a rifle went off accidentally. The Tibetans, thinking they were about to be attacked, drew their swords and flung themselves on the column. The troops opened fire; and from two sides of a square, volley after volley thudded into the close-packed bodies

of the Tibetans. They didn't break and run. They simply turned their backs on the barricade and, with head bowed, *walked* through the hail of bullets. Within minutes, six hundred lay dead or dying. "I hope," wrote one of the young British officers in a letter to his mother, "that I shall never again have to shoot men who are *walking* away." Younghusband was appalled. "It was," he wrote, "a terrible and ghastly business."

The road to Lhasa lay open. But at what a price.

There were several more skirmishes in the weeks that followed. But when it came to fighting, the Tibetans were no match for Macdonald's Gurkhas and Sikhs. Indeed the main obstacle to the last stage of the British advance turned out to be the Brahmaputra River, now swollen by monsoon rain. The Brahmaputra was crossed at the end of July; and on August 2nd the British "diplomatic mission" arrived at its journey's end. Lhasa. *"The goal of so many travellers' ambitions was in sight,"* wrote Younghusband. *"The goal to attain which we had endured and risked so much. Every obstacle which nature and man combined to heap in our way had been overcome, and the sacred city, hidden so far and deep behind the Himalayan ramparts, and so jealously guarded from strangers, lay before our eyes."*

The arrival of foreign troops in Lhasa marked the end of an era. For centuries the

"The Dalai Lama as a God": a painting in the Potala photographed by L.A. Waddell, the expedition's doctor. The Dalai Lama has been described as "the pope of Tibet", the guardian of Tibetan Buddhism who is believed never to die but to transmigrate miraculously from one body to another. As long ago as 1886 the Indian explorer Nain Singh wrote prophetically: "The Tibetans have need of such a Lama to prevent the government of their country falling into the hands of the Chinese."

"Forbidden City" had been veiled in mystery. This veil was now torn aside, and Lhasa lay revealed to the outside world for what it was – a city of bizarre contrasts: the wealth of its monasteries contrasting with the poverty of its people, the beauty of its setting contrasting with the squalor of its buildings, and the good nature of its people contrasting with their sudden bouts of appalling cruelty. For nearly a thousand years Tibet had preserved its independence for the simple reason that it had preserved its isolation. The end of isolation meant the end of independence.

Ironically, it was not the British who gained from the ending of Tibet's isolation. It was the Chinese. For as Younghusband and his troops approached Lhasa, the Dalai Lama fled; and it was China he fled to. Younghusband negotiated a treaty with the Tibetan officials who had been left behind. In the short-term the treaty may have brought benefits to Britain; but in the long-term it proved a disaster. For what happened was this. The treaty made a point of excluding Russian troops, agents and traders from Tibet. The British, however, were not prepared to garrison the country themselves. Tibet was therefore left in a sort of vacuum. This suited the Chinese very well; and when in 1906 the Dalai Lama returned to Lhasa, he returned with Chinese troops and Chinese backing.

The British had saved Tibet from the Bear, only to hand it over to the Dragon!

Since 1906 Tibet has been, for much of the time, under Chinese suzerainty. The Chinese have done many good things in Tibet. The Tibetan people are now living in the present not the past, and their old feudal hierarchy has been swept away. Unhappily, a lot of good things have been swept away with the bad. Tibetan monasteries have been desecrated; Tibetan sacred texts have been used to floor public lavatories; prayer-wheels no longer hum; the Dalai Lama has fled to India. It is a matter of opinion whether the advantages of Chinese suzerainty outweigh the disadvantages or *vice versa*: whether the search for the "Forbidden City" ended in triumph or in tragedy.

3 The Great Game

Younghusband's mission to Lhasa has been described as "one of the last moves in the Great Game." The Great Game was the name given – half jokingly, half in earnest – to the power struggle in central Asia between the empires of Great Britain and Imperial Russia.

Throughout the 19th century the mountains of central Asia were like a no-man's land between the rival British and Russian empires. The British were pushing their way into the mountains from the south. The Russians were pushing their way into the mountains from the north. In the east other and older players of the Game, the Chinese, were watching and waiting. It was a scenario that didn't encourage exploration. For every explorer who ventured into the mountains was suspected – often quite rightly – of being a spy. Spies, throughout history, have met violent and mysterious deaths. And this is what happened to one of the earliest and greatest players of the Great Game, William Moorcroft.

Moorcroft was nearly sixty years old when, in 1819, he set out on an amazing five-year journey which was to take him from Lahore in India to Bukhara in the U.S.S.R. In the early stages of his journey he faced the suspicion and hostility of the Sikhs. In the middle stages he faced the suspicion and hostility of the Chinese; and in the latter stages he faced the suspicion and hostility of the Russians. Moorcroft had no official backing. He was manager of one of the East India Company's stud farms, and was supposed to be buying horses. Unofficially, however, he negotiated and signed treaties and did everything possible to extend the British sphere of influence. No wonder that on more than one occasion he was attacked and imprisoned. It is anyone's guess who finally murdered him in the deserts of present-day Turkmenskaya.

The next victims of the Great Game were Charles Stoddart and Arthur Conolly. Stoddart and Conolly were British army officers who, in 1838, were sent to Bukhara to offer the local ruler protection against the Russians. The local ruler, however, decided he didn't need protecting, and Stoddart and Conolly ended up in the *Siah Cha* ("black well"): a horrible, six-metre deep pit in which were kept specially-bred ticks, snakes and reptiles which lived on human flesh. For several years Stoddart and Conolly were hauled in and out of the pit like yo-yos. Stoddart saw his grave being dug in front of him, and was given the choice of becoming a Moslem or being burned alive . . . In 1842 an eccentric British clergyman, Joseph Wolff, set out on a quixotic mission to try and save Stoddart and Conolly. After an arduous journey Wolff also ended up in Bukhara – and in the *Siah Cha*! He learned that the two officers had been publicly executed, and was told the same fate awaited him. *"One morning,"* Wolff wrote, *"a mulla came to my cell with a message: was I prepared to become a Moslem? 'Tell the ruler NEVER, NEVER, NEVER', I replied. Next day there came the executioner who had put Stoddart and Conolly to death. 'Joseph Wolff,' he said, 'to thee it shall happen as it did to Stoddart and Conolly'. As he spoke he made a sign at my throat with his hand. I prepared for death, and carried opium always with me. But at the last I cast away the opium and prayed."* A few days later Wolff was unexpectedly released, laden with presents, and told he could go home. It is pleasant to record that he owed his freedom, at least in part, to the pleading of Colonel Butenyov, the Russian political agent in Bukhara. Butenyov was no friend of the British: but he seems to have been so sickened by the local ruler's cruelty that he did everything he could to get Stoddart, Conolly and Wolff released. In the case of Wolff he succeeded.

The next important player of the Great Game to explore the mountains was Godfrey Thomas Vigne. Vigne would have us believe that he was a simple sportsman and artist; and it is true

"Kashmir the equal of Paradise." This picture of the Sind Valley by Major Molyneux makes us realise why artists as well as explorers were attracted to the Vale of Kashmir.

he had a passion for hunting, and a considerable talent for painting – several of his sketches were exhibited by the Royal Academy. In the late 1830s Vigne arrived in northwest India, and at once disappeared into the unknown. He was to spend the next five years in the mountains, and was certainly the first European to explore the Vale of Kashmir and probably the first to set eyes on the Karakoram. But were his travels purely for pleasure? Or was he a spy? What makes me suspect the latter is that he spent so much of his time exploring the passes which lead into and out of the Vale of Kashmir. It was of course these passes (the potential invasion-routes) which the British authorities were anxious to know about. Whatever his motives, Vigne was one of the few travellers of his generation to have a genuine rapport with the people of Kashmir and Baltistan, and a genuine love of their country. He describes the Vale of Kashmir as *"the noblest valley in all the world, well worthy of the epithets Kashmir bi nuzir* (Kashmir without equal) *and Kashmir junat puzir* (Kashmir the equal of Paradise)"; while his books contain some of the finest descriptions of the Karakoram that have ever been written. He was also one of the few players of the Great Game to survive.

Another survivor of the Game was John Wood. Wood was a tough, laconic naval lieutenant who had traced much of the course of the River Indus, and was determined to do the same for the Amu-Daria. The Amu-Daria is one of the world's great rivers, "a lifeline thrown down by Allah to the desert people when they were dying of thirst"; however, its source, like that of the Nile, remained a mystery almost up to the middle of the 19th century. Wood got himself attached to a political mission in Kunduz, a town on the north-facing slopes of the Hindu Kush. He then managed to obtain permission from the local ruler to search for the source of the Amu-Daria.

Seldom can so important a journey have been undertaken with so little fuss. *"Monday 11th December, 1837,"* Wood wrote, *"was fortunately a market-day in Kunduz; so the articles required for our expedition were at once obtained; and, lest the ruler withdraw his permission, we started off the same evening. We adopted the costume of the country, and had little baggage. Coarse clothes to barter for food were our sole stock in trade, and my chronometers were the only articles of value I took with me."* Wood's journey took him into the desolate plateau where the Hindu Kush, the Pamir, the Karakoram and the Himalayas come together in a jumble of high valleys and higher peaks. It was winter. Conditions were always difficult and often impossible. After travelling a couple of hundred kilometres in search of the upper reaches of the Amu-Daria, Wood found himself unable to make progress against the bitter winds and snow driven off the Pamir. The temperature dropped to $-32°C$, and in the little town of Jerm Wood was forced by blizzards to lie up for nearly a month. Setting out again, he struggled to the top of a 3,000-metre pass. Here he met a solitary traveller, encased from head to foot in the skin of a horse. Unable to ride his horse through deepening snow, the traveller had killed it, skinned it, and continued his journey on foot encased against the cold in the animal's hide. Reaching the top of the pass, Wood stood staring down on a scene of utter desolation: a snowscape silent and lifeless as the face of the moon. Of the Amu-Daria there was no sign; like everything else it lay hidden under the snow. When Wood did at last stumble across the river, he found it had "burst its winter fetters", and become a torrent of churning blocks of ice covered with unstable bridges of snow. Conditions became so terrible that his native companions refused to go a step farther. Wood, however, wouldn't admit defeat. He appealed to a group of nomadic Kirghiz who happened to be camped nearby. The Kirghiz were a warlike people, who had the reputation of cutting off strangers' ears, if not their heads. Wood, however, walked boldly into one of their yurts (tents) and asked if they would act as his guides. His courage was rewarded. Next day, together with thirteen companions mounted on yaks, Wood set out for the *Bam-i-Duniah*, 'the roof of the world', where according to Kirghiz legend the Amu-Daria had its source in a lake surrounded by eternally snow-capped mountains. It was so cold that the mercury disappeared into the bulb at the bottom of Wood's thermometer. His yaks fell through the ice and into the river. The Kirghiz suffered from frostbite and gave up one by one. But Wood, who must have been among the most physically tough of all explorers, kept going, until he came at last to his journey's end, Lake Sir-i-kol. *"In the afternoon of 19th February,"* he wrote, *"we stood upon the* Bam-i-Duniah, *and saw before us a noble frozen sheet of water, from whose western end issued the infant river. On three sides the lake is bounded by swelling hills; whilst along its southern flanks are mountains rising some 3,500 feet (1,050 metres) above the lake, or 19,000 feet (6,000 metres) above the sea. These mountains are covered with perpetual snow, from which never-failing source the lake is supplied . . . Wherever the eye fell one dazzling sheet of snow carpeted the ground. The sky was dark blue. Clouds would have been welcome to the eye, but they were wanting. Not a breath of wind moved over the surface of the lake; not a beast nor a bird was visible. Silence reigned – a silence so profound that it oppressed the heart."* Lake Sir-i-kol is one of the loneliest places on Earth.

After discovering the source of the Amu-Daria, Wood returned immediately to England. It was as well for him he did. For the British players of the Great Game were about to suffer a major disaster – the Afghan Wars of 1841/42. During these wars British garrisons, British expeditions and British political agents were massacred, sometimes literally to the last man; and Wood was lucky to escape the holocaust. The Afghan Wars led to the annexation of the Punjab; and this in turn led to a vast new mountain-area being opened up to explorers.

It so happened that just at the time the Punjab was being annexed, British surveyors were working their way towards the mountains from the south. These surveyors were attached to the Great Trigonometrical Survey of India – one of the most ambitious and important geographical projects the world has ever known. Early in the 19th century Sir George Everest, the Surveyor-General of India succeeded in measuring accurately the great meridional arc (or great circle) which passes through the centre of India. This arc was then used as the basis from which the position and height of all the other places in India could be calculated. What happened was this. On the top of a mountain whose height was known, Everest's surveyors would build an observation post. From here they would take bearings on the unknown peaks ahead. They would then climb another mountain whose height was known, and from here take bearings on the same peaks from another direction. The resulting network of triangulation would enable them to work out the exact position and the exact height of the unknown peaks. Here is an account of how William Johnson, probably the greatest of the surveyors, set up one of his observation posts in the Himalayas. *"Wood and provisions had to be sent on ahead, and sufficient labourers had to accompany the party to clear away the snow, then build the platform and masonary pillar, and construct a hut for the lamp-men . . . After a difficult climb over the snow, ascending on the last day no less than 7,000 feet (2,100 metres), Mr. Johnson reached the summit. In choosing a site for the* (observation) *post he naturally selected the highest part of the snow. It was found, however, that this was not the highest part of the mountain; for even after removing an enormous quantity of snow, no solid rock could be perceived. Another part of the summit was then tried; and here, fortunately, rock was found within 11 feet (3 metres) of the surface of the snow. Here building was commenced . . . The working-party, however, were soon surrounded by a thin cloud, so charged with electricity that their hair and clothing crackled and emitted sparks. This electricity, added to snow-blindness, headaches* (caused by altitude sickness) *and cold, made work difficult. But after much labour a platform and pillar were finished, and a hut constructed. After staying for several days on the peak, much hindered by cloud and snowstorms, Mr. Johnson took the necessary observations and was able to descend safely."*

Johnson's career with the Great Trigonometrical Survey ended in 1865 when he crossed a range too far, and started mapping the Chinese side of the border. This triggered off an international incident, and Johnson was summarily dismissed. Like his *Khalasis*

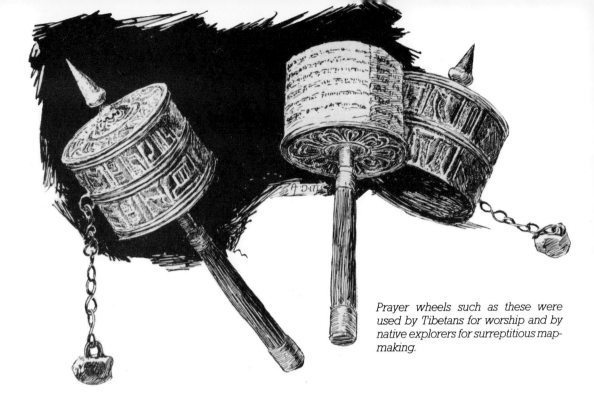

Prayer wheels such as these were used by Tibetans for worship and by native explorers for surreptitious map-making.

(native-born surveyors) he has seldom been given the recognition he deserves.

The trouble caused by Johnson's entry into China highlights one of the great difficulties British surveyors had to face. They were denied access to many of the ranges they wanted to explore. Eventually Johnson's boss, Thomas Montgomerie, hit on the idea of training Indians – who were less likely to be recognised than Europeans – as surveyors. These Indians were taught to walk at a uniform 2,000 paces to the mile (1.6 kilometres), and to keep note of how many paces they took. They were also taught how to calculate latitude and height. They were then disguised as traders or pilgrims, and sent into the mountains to make secret route-surveys of the territories beyond the frontier.

In a paper read to the Royal Geographical Society, Montgomerie describes some of the tricks these native explorers got up to. *"I had noticed the frequent use made by Tibetans of the rosary and the prayer-wheel, and recommended my Pundits* (as the native-born explorers were called) *to carry both, especially as it was thought these instruments could be useful in carrying out a route survey. It was necessary that Pundits should be able to take compass bearings unobserved, and that when counting their paces they should not be interrupted. Pundit Nain Singh found it best to march separately . . . and when people did come up to him, the sight of his prayer-wheel was sufficient to stop them addressing him. For when he saw anyone approaching, he at once began to whirl his wheel round; and as all good Buddhists doing this are supposed to be in religious contemplation, he was seldom disturbed. The prayer-wheel used was an ordinary hand one; but inside it, instead of the usual Buddhist prayer Om mani padme hum* ('Hail, oh jewel in the lotus'), *were slips of paper for recording bearings etc. The Pundits' rosaries, instead of the usual 108 beads, had 100, every tenth bead being larger than the others . . . at every 100th pace a bead was dropped. Each large bead to fall therefore represented 1000 paces, or half a mile (.8 kilometres). Observations of latitude were difficult. Artificial horizons of dark glass were provided; but the use of quicksilver (mercury) was found more satisfactory . . . Quicksilver is difficult to carry; but Nain Singh managed to hide his by putting some in a cocoa-nut, and by carrying his reserve in cowrie shells sealed with wax."*

The best known of the Pundits is probably Nain Singh, whose epic journey to Lhasa earned him the distinction of being the first non-European to be awarded the Gold Medal of the Royal Geographical Society. But to my mind the most amazing of all the Pundits' journeys was that of the explorer Kinthup.

We don't know much about Kinthup. We don't know where or when he was born. We don't even know his first name. We do, however, know that in 1880 he was given the task of solving the mystery of the Tsangpo and Brahmaputra Rivers. The Tsangpo was known to flow east across the plateau of Tibet. The Brahmaputra was known to flow south onto the plains of India. But nobody knew if the Tsangpo and the Brahmaputra were one and the same river or two separate rivers; for there was a 200 kilometre gap between them so steep, rocky, rain-sodden and fiercely-guarded that no European had been able to explore it. In 1879 Captain Harman of the Royal Engineers suggested that a number of specially marked logs of wood should be thrown into the Tsangpo, and that a watch should be kept for these logs on the Brahmaputra. Kinthup was given the task of throwing in the logs. And what a task it turned out to be!

In order to reach the Tsangpo, Kinthup had first to penetrate the forbidden territory of Tibet. He decided to travel disguised as the servant of a Mongolian lama who was visiting relatives in Lhasa. He and the lama set out in August 1880 and had no great difficulty reaching the Tibetan capital, where the lama at any rate thoroughly enjoyed himself, *"feasting non-stop for six days with his colleagues in the monastery"*. By mid-September the two travellers were following the Tsangpo east over the barren plateau of Tibet. The weather became worse. The terrain became increasingly rugged. The river became increasingly difficult to follow. They found the Nga La Pass *"knee-deep in snow, and the wind so violent* (they) *could scarce crawl against it on hands and knees."* By now it was obvious that the lama was regretting he had got himself involved in so hazardous a venture. We are told that *"at a place called Thun Tsung he fell in love with the wife of his host, and could in no way be persuaded to continue the journey."* As a result of the lama's *amours*, the travellers were delayed for four months. What was worse, they had to pay their host *"25 rupees in compensation"*. So when they did at last set off once again down the Tsangpo, they barely had sufficient money to pay the tolls which were demanded each time they crossed a bridge over the river. By the time they reached a town called Tongjuk Dzong they had no money left.

Exactly what happened at Tongjuk Dzong will probably never be known. It seems, however, that one morning the lama ordered Kinthup not to leave the house of the Tibetan official with whom they were lodging. The lama then rode off on a horse which he had somehow acquired. Kinthup never saw him again. It was only gradually that the Pundit realised what had happened. The lama, in exchange for the horse, had sold him into slavery.

There is no evidence that the Tibetans treated Kinthup badly – he seems to have spent most of his time making clothes or cutting grass. He was, however, kept strictly in servitude; and only after seven months of drudgery was he able to escape. A less dedicated man would have run for home. Kinthup, however, was determined to carry out his mission. He therefore set off down the Tsangpo. It was a hard journey. In some places he had to follow the river as it rushed down dangerous rapids. In other places he had to fight his way across sodden thickly-forested mountains. Knowing that the Tibetans were likely to be on the lookout for him, he avoided villages, and slept each night in caves or fissures among the rocks. However, there were times when he had no option but to cross the river by bridge; and at one such bridge his master and his servants caught up with him. Kinthup fled to a nearby monastery. He flung himself at the head lama's feet, and begged for mercy. The head lama bargained with Kinthup's master, and eventually bought the Pundit for 50 rupees – though it isn't clear whether this was out of pity for him, or because he reckoned he was cheap at the price!

Kinthup served his new master for nearly

The Kinthup Falls on the Brahmaputra, named after the Pundit explorer.

five months. He was then given temporary leave to make a pilgrimage. However, instead of visiting the holy shrines as he had promised to do, he made his way once again down the Tsangpo. When he came to a lonely, uninhabited part of the river, he began to cut logs. He cut five hundred logs in five days. Each log was exactly one foot (30 centimetres) long and specially notched. Kinthup hid his logs in a deep cave beside the river. Then he returned to his master the lama.

He returned to the lama because by this time it was long past the date when he ought to have thrown his logs into the Tsangpo, and he was afraid that the watch for them would have been called off. He therefore decided to try to get a message back to Captain Harman, advising him of a new date for launching the logs. Such a message, he knew, could only be sent

via Lhasa. He therefore served the lama for a further two months, before asking permission to make yet another pilgrimage, this time to the holy mountain of Tsari. Impressed by such piety, the lama granted his request. So Kinthup again left the monastery. But instead of heading for Tsari, he headed for Lhasa.

We have no details of Kinthup's journey to Lhasa. The only account that we have of it is a somewhat scrappy report, written years later by a Colonel Tanner of the Indian Army. The colonel tells us little except that: *"the Pundit slept at nights on hard ground. The ground was covered with snow . . . There were no shelters except the occasional cave . . . The road was bad, and so steep not even a mule could climb it."* When, at last, Kinthup struggled into Lhasa, he had been working as a slave for fifteen months, and sleeping rough on one of the highest and bleakest plateaux in the world for a further fifteen months. A lesser man would have taken the opportunity to escape to India. Kinthup, however, was *still* determined to carry out his orders. He therefore made contact with an official from Sikkim who was visiting one of the monasteries, and persuaded him to take back a letter addressed to the Surveyor-General. *"Sir,"* the letter read, *"the lama who was sent with me sold me as a slave, and himself fled away . . . On account of this, the journey proved a bad one. However, I, Kinthup, have prepared the 500 logs according to the orders of Captain Harman, and am preparing to throw 50 logs per day into the Tsang-po at Bipung, from the 5th to the 15th of the tenth Tibetan month of the year."* Kinthup impressed on the official the importance of delivering the letter to the Surveyor-General, then set out yet again for the monastery to complete his term of slavery to the lama.

Tanner dismisses the events of the next year in a single paragraph. *"Crossing the Tsang-po the Pundit . . . retraced his route and went back to the Lama, and again served under him for 9 months. At the end of 9 months the Lama set him free, saying, 'I am glad to see you visiting the sacred places, so from today I give you leave to go anywhere you like.' Kinthup bowed thrice before him, and bid him good-bye thankfully. After a month he made his way to*

Bipung, where he stayed 10 days, and threw his 500 logs into the Tsang-po. He spent one month longer by the river, in order to earn enough money to buy food for his journey back to India . . . He returned to his village in September, 1884, after an absence of more than 1,500 days."

How one wishes that Kinthup's perserverance had been rewarded; but the Pundit, alas, seems to have been a born loser. Arriving home, he found that his mother had just died. Arriving in Darjeeling, he found that his letter to the Surveyor-General had never been delivered. No watch had been kept for his logs, and they had drifted unseen into the Bay of Bengal. The link between the Tsangpo and the Brahmaputra still hadn't been proved. Worst of all, Captain Harman had also died, and

Below: The British and Russian officers of the Pamir Boundary Commission (Colonel Holdich on the extreme right).

Kinthup's report of his adventures was not believed. It was several years before it was realised that every bit of information he brought back was nothing but the truth. By this time Kinthup had vanished.

Kinthup was a typical Pundit, one of those unselfish, unrewarded men whose journeys were so secret that even today little is known about them. What we *do* know, however, is that the Pundits – like the Hindu pilgrims and the native-born *Khalasis* – were great explorers. The role played by the people of the Indian sub-continent in exploring their mountains should not be underestimated.

The end of the 19th century saw one of the last and most ironic moves in the Great Game. For years British and Russian players of the Game had been using the mountains as a sort of chessboard: capturing strongholds, strengthening their position by alliance, subterfuge and murder, all for the sake of advancing their frontier. Yet when the frontier

was at last agreed, the British officer in charge of marking it out could write: *"It is a matter of indifference exactly where it is drawn."* While of the Russians, who for years had been such bogeymen, he could say: *"They are grand chaps. I acknowledge both the excellence of their mapping and the warmth of their hospitality."* This unexpected rapport between the Lion and the Bear was brought about by the Pamir Boundary Commission.

The Pamir Boundary Commission had two objectives. First, to settle the actual line of the frontier and mark it with masonary pillars. Second to bring about *"a junction with the Russian survey-system which would provide a common basis for the mapping of central Asia."* The team entrusted with these tasks needed to be both surveyors and diplomats. They needed, too, to be competent mountaineers; for the survey teams planned to meet on the shore of Wood's bleak and isolated Lake Sir-i-kol, and mark out the frontier together across the very Roof of the World.

The British team consisted of five officers, eighteen native surveyors, an escort of nineteen native troops, and two hundred ponies. They set out from the Vale of Kashmir in June, 1895. There is a saying "it is more blessed to travel than to arrive". Many expeditions have found the approaches to the great peaks every bit as satisfying as the peaks themselves; and certainly that summer the road to the Pamir seemed touched with magic. Colonel Holdich, one of the officers on the expedition, gives us an excellent account of the beauties and difficulties of their journey. *"Kashmir in summer. Surely there is no place like it! Our track ran through close-set lanes bordered with hedges of wild rose and passion flower. Cornflower and poppy were in bloom in the fields, and the little orchards with their turf sloping green to the river's edge, presented a most beautiful picture. Darkot is particularly picturesque. For here the well-cultivated fields and orchards are enclosed in a mighty surrounding wall of granite and limestone mountains, up whose sides wind some of the grandest glacial staircases in the world . . . The way ahead seemed closed . . . But there is a way out of Darkot: a dangerous climb over broken moraine and fissured glacier, until one arrives at the snowfields of the Darkot pass, fifteen thousand feet (4,500 metres) above sea level. By the time we got over the pass nearly all our party were snowblind. But the few of us who could see were rewarded by a glorious scene: a great array of peaks, white with new-fallen snow. Here at the summit of the pass our surveyors made their first observations to carry the Indian triangulation over the Hindu Kush."* To the north of the pass lay the Wakhan Valley: *"a devil's pathway zigzagging between gigantic icebound spurs."* This was difficult country through which to travel, and it was mid-July before the expedition emerged onto the more open plains of the Pamir. This was a world of high winds, high rounded valleys, and even higher domelike peaks. It was a harsh land, but travelling was relatively easy. By July 22nd – the exact date provisionally agreed for a rendezvous with the Russians – the British surveyors were nearing Lake Sir-i-kol. *"About two miles* (three kilometres) *from the lake,"* writes Holdich, *"we were met by a detachment of Cossacks bearing torches on the end of their lances to light us into their camp."* The British officers, in the best tradition of the day, had intended changing for dinner. *"But the Russian Commissioner would accept no excuse for delay, insisting that our dusty party ride on to the Russian camp at once. Here we were received with the most courteous hospitality, and the foundation was laid for that good fellowship between the two camps which never was broken."* Much vodka was drunk that night. Many promises were made – and none of them broken.

In the weeks that followed, British and Russian surveyors worked side by side. They found that although the British survey had started 3,000 kilometres away in Madras, and the Russian survey had started 4,800 kilometres away in Leningrad, when their maps were joined together they were in near-miraculous agreement. *"At the end of all our triangulation we found ourselves standing together on the roof of the world with practically no difference between us to eliminate – surely a cause for mutual congratulation!"* The accuracy with which both nations had carried out their surveys made fixing the position of the frontier relatively easy. Indeed the main problem was the weather: day after day of sleet, with high winds and heavy banks of cloud obscuring the ranges. But by September 7th, the final pillar was raised into position. It was an historic moment. *"Here,"* wrote Holdich, *"amidst a vast white wilderness 20,000 feet (6,000 metres) above the sea, inaccessible to man and known to no living creature except the Pamir eagles, the British, Russian and Chinese empires come together. It is a fit meeting place. No god of mythology ever occupied a more stupendous throne."*

Their work completed, the British and the Russians staged "such a party as the Pamir had never before seen." The afternoon was given over to feats of horsemanship, including a game of *Buzgali bazi*, played by the local Kirghiz. *"This is a game,"* Holdich tells us, *"common to all High Asia. It consists of a savage fight by mounted horsemen for the possession of a goat (dead or alive) which is carried by one of the performers. The object of the goat-carrier is to retain possession of the carcass, to ride clear of all opposition, and deposit the carcass in a sanctuary (a selected space of open ground). The game was fast, furious and reckless. Dust rose in thick clouds over the spinning horsemen. In the heat of the fray, horses and men plunged headlong into the river, and it seemed due only to some special Kirghiz providence that they ever came out again."* What Holdich *doesn't* tell us is that not so many years ago the game of *Buzgali bazi* was played not with a goat but with a prisoner-of-war: a prisoner who was alive at the start of the game, but by the end was torn literally limb from limb. The night was given over to drinking and dancing, by the light of a huge bonfire. *"Wood,"* writes Holdich, *"had been collected from valleys south of the Hindu Kush and brought with us as a provision against having to spend winter in the Pamir. All this wood was now stacked into such a bonfire as the Pamir will never see again, and round about it various dances were conducted with much energy and spirit. Grog was brewed in a vast Russian cauldron, and nothing could exceed the enthusiasm with which the*

The game Buzgali bazi is played throughout High Asia and has changed little over the centuries.

toast 'Entente cordiale' between our countries was received. Music was provided by pipes, a concertina and a Kerosine tin drum. The night was still, and as cold as 25° of frost could make it; and the moonlight glinting on the freezing surface of the river and marsh added to the fantastic effect of the scene."

Next morning the Russians mounted their camels and headed west. The British mounted their Kashmiri ponies and headed east. And *"the Pamir were left to their eternal silence and the fragments of our still-smoking bonfire."*

A month later the British surveyors were back in the Vale of Kashmir. Their mission had been a success. Not a man had been lost. The survey of India had been extended over the Hindu Kush and into the heart of the Pamir; and a frontier which had been in dispute for eighty years had been agreed and marked out. But even more important than what was done was the spirit in which it was done. For when, at the end of the road, the players of the Great Game met face to face, there were no quarrels, no disputes, no tension. Just a group of ordinary men doing a job together, relaxing together, and finding they liked one another. I had the same experience myself, with the Russians whom I met in Murmansk during the Second World War. Perhaps there is a lesson here from which politicians could learn.

4 The First Climbers

Mountaineering as a pastime started in the European Alps less than a couple of hundred years ago. Before that, no-one thought of climbing for pleasure. In 1865 climbers reached the summit of the most difficult of the European Alps, the Matterhorn. They then began to look for fresh peaks to conquer, and it wasn't long before they became interested in the Himalayas.

The first person to come to the Himalayas, in his own words, "purely to climb and purely for sport and adventure," was the Englishman, W.W. Graham. Graham arrived in Nepal in 1883. He made a number of brave and skilful climbs, but soon found that the Himalayas were a far tougher proposition than the Alps. The reports which Graham sent back to Europe were read with interest by both climbers and scientists. Scientists were particularly interested in Graham's reports because it was about this time that people were making a scientific and systematic study of the world. Scientists therefore wanted to know all about the mountains: not only how high they were, but what rocks they were made of, and what forces had fashioned them. Mountaineering expeditions began to be planned with a dual objective: to climb some unconquered peak, *and* to add to mankind's store of knowledge.

This new aspect of mountaineering, the search for knowledge, was of special interest to the Royal Geographical Society. This Society had been founded in 1830 with the broad objective of promoting geography and geographical research. In the past it had sponsored explorers like Franklin, Livingstone, Burton and Speke. In the future it was to sponsor not only explorers like Scott, Shackleton and Fuchs, but also mountaineers like Shipton, Hunt and Chris Bonington. In 1892 the Society launched its first major mountaineering expedition, Martin Conway's reconnaissance of the great glaciers of the Karakoram. This reconnaissance was the forerunner of a whole series of expeditions sponsored by the Society. These expeditions reached their climax in 1953 with Hillary and Tenzing triumphant on the summit of Everest – their ascent having been masterminded, down to the last detail, from the Society's headquarters in London. Nor is this the end of the story. For every year *since* 1953, the Society has supported more than one major scientific project among the great peaks of the world.

Conway's expedition arrived in Pakistan in the spring of 1892. Their aim was *"to explore and survey the glacial area of the Karakoram and in particular the great Baltoro Glacier . . . also to make a determined attempt to climb one of the loftier peaks."* Conway and his team pioneered a pattern of mountaineering which was to be repeated many times by many expeditions in the years to come. First, the long trek, with columns of porters, through the foothills. Then the reconnaissance, and the setting up of a base camp at the foot of the mountain they hoped to climb. Then the "laying siege" to that mountain, with a succession of tents being pushed ever higher up its untrodden slopes. And finally the assault – which was often unsuccessful! – on the summit.

During his trek through the foothills Conway had two problems: his porters and the weather. His expedition was a large one, more than a hundred men carrying more than 2,250 kilograms of equipment and food. Some of his porters came from Nepal, some from Kashmir and some from Baltistan; they spoke seven different languages, and getting them to work happily together was no easy task. To start with there was friction and non-co-operation. *"The local men,"* wrote Conway, *"are a rotten lot, always wanting to lay down their packs and run"*. Things, however, got better; and this was due largely to Conway's second-in-command, Lieutenant (later General) Bruce. Bruce believed in leading by example. *"We came to a stream,"* wrote Conway, *"which was so swollen by the monsoon rain that our endeavours to cross it were for a long time fruitless. Eventually a Gurkha managed to cross it*

Martin Conway, leader of the first British mountaineering expedition to the Karakoram, and the Golden Throne (Baltoro Kangri) which he attempted to climb.

with a climbing rope. With this fastened from bank to bank, and the Gurkhas and Bruce standing thigh-deep in the icy stream to help, we at last managed to get the porters across. The stream was rising all the time, and the last to cross were buried up to their chests in the swift torrent. Bruce was here, there and everywhere, with his usual energy. He himself carried over almost half the sheep, taking them one by one under his right arm, while with his left he grasped the rope." By the time they arrived at the Karakoram, the porters would follow Bruce anywhere.

Conway's other problem, the weather, was not solved so easily. He had arrived at the worst possible time, at the height of the summer monsoon. Rain fell without respite; and as his expedition neared the mountains they were driven back by huge and terrible avalanches, which cascaded almost hourly off the peaks. However, by 1st August conditions had slightly improved, and Conway and his team were camped at the foot of the Baltoro Glacier. The trek was over. The reconnaissance was about to begin.

Conway's first impressions of the Baltoro were not favourable. The lower part of the glacier consisted of "mile after mile of horrible stone-covered slopes of ice . . . There can't be anything in the world more loathsome, monotonous or fatiguing to travel over . . . Undoubtedly this glacier far surpasses in discomfort anything that any of us have known." Surveying was hampered by sleet and low cloud. However, after nearly a week of slow and difficult progress, Conway and his men were rewarded by the gradual unfolding, ahead of them, of some spectacular scenery. For in its upper reaches the Baltoro opens out, and is flanked and headed by some of the most beautiful mountains on Earth. "First Gusherbrum (8,073m) disclosed his giant tower ahead of us . . . The evening of the (next) day revealed the glorious Masherbrum (7,826m) his summit golden in the sunlight, and his grand skirts of snow sweeping down to the glacier." While on August 10th there rose at the head of the valley "an enormous mountain, not marked on any map. It was throne-like in form, and yellow veins seemed to permeate its mass; we there-

fore named it the Golden Throne (Baltoro Kangri, 7,134m). As we gazed at this most beautiful mountain, revealed in the mixed light of moon and dawn, we cried, 'That is the peak for us. That one we will climb, and no other'." The expedition set up their base camp at the foot of Baltoro Kangri. The reconnaissance was over. The climbing was about to begin.

Conway had written that "the (Karakoram) peaks are difficult in their lower parts, but the regions above 17,000 feet (5,000 metres) look easy." He was soon to be disillusioned. His team spent several days surveying the upper reaches of the Baltoro; then, in what was to become the classic style of big expeditions, they laid siege to the mountain of their dreams. A base camp (Junction Camp) was established at about 4,000 metres, close to the moraine of a small glacier. A couple of days later Camp I (Footstool Camp) was set up at roughly 5,000 metres, "in a magnificent position, at the foot of the precipices guarding Baltoro Kangri, with a peak of over 25,000 feet (7,500 metres) on either side of us." A week later they had stockpiled these two camps with food, and established Camp II (Serac Camp) at a height of nearly 5,500 metres. Then their troubles started. "Dawn on the 21st broke lurid and threatening. An ominous orange glow rested on the higher peaks, and illuminated the wild clouds that swirled about them. The weather was about to break." Next day Bruce and one of the Gurkhas succumbed to altitude sickness, and had to be helped down to a lower camp. By the time they had established Camp III (Upper Plateau Camp) at a little over 6,000 metres, all the climbers were suffering from frostbite, headaches brought about by lack of oxygen, and a depressing lassitude. "After lacing up a boot, one has to lie down and take several deep breaths before attempting to lace the next." They were still a fair way below the summit. Conway, however, decided to make a dash for it.

They set out at six in the morning. Within half-an-hour their feet were so frostbitten that they had lost all feeling. The rising sun, however, brought them temporary relief. They struggled on, up slopes which may have *looked* easy, but which turned out to be very much the opposite. *"Beyond the col,"* writes Conway, *"there was a very steep face of mingled ice and rock which had to be surmounted. We had a tough scramble for a quarter-of-an-hour, then expected better things. But, to our horror, we found that the ridge leading to the summit was not of snow but of hard blue ice. Every step we took had to be cut. Zurbriggen* (their Swiss guide) *found the work of step-cutting far more fatiguing than at the European levels . . . The ascent was monotonous. The white ridge led straight up in front of us, and had to be followed. Here again every step had to be cut. Also the ridge was heavily corniced* (overhung) *to our left, so we were forced to keep to the right-hand slope, and were ignorant of the view on the other side. Our advance was slow, and the heat which the burning rays of the sun poured upon us, did nothing to add to its rapidity. It was as though we were in the middle of an area of utter aerial stagnation. I heard the click-click of Zurbriggen's axe making steps, and struggled mechanically from one to another, only dimly conscious of the vast depths below us. Then the slope became less steep. A few more steps and we were on the summit. But here a most unwelcome surprise awaited us. The summit of the Golden Throne was still nearly 400 metres above us, and the peak on which we stood was absolutely cut off from it by a deep depression. We had climbed another mountain!"*

In the years to come this mistake was to be repeated many times by climbers attempting the great peaks of the Himalayas and the Karakoram. Conway's error was understandable. He and his men spent an hour on the summit, surveying and taking photographs. They also carried out rough and ready medical tests, and found that their pulse rates were dangerously high and their hearts dangerously strained. They hadn't a hope, Conway realised, of reaching the summit of the Golden Throne and getting back alive. *"There was,"* he wrote, *"no debate about what we should do next. Nothing remained for us but downward and homeward."*

A couple of months later his expedition was back in England. By and large it had a been a success. The longest glacier in the world outside the polar ice-caps had been mapped; new peaks had been discovered, and Conway had climbed higher than anyone had ever climbed before. Useful scientific information had been brought back, and useful experience had been gained. But it was the president of the Royal Geographical Society, Douglas Freshfield, who put his finger on what was perhaps the expedition's greatest achievement. *"I am sure,"* he said, *"that Mr. Conway's exploits will have the effect of interesting the Indians themselves in mountaineering . . . If we can teach these people to act as mountain guides, we shall have solved the problem of the exploration of the Himalayas."* Freshfield was right. For virtually all the great peaks of the Himalayas and the Karakoram were first climbed by expeditions which owed their success to their native porters and climbers.

Conway had enjoyed a good relationship with his porters. It was a different story with our next explorers, the Workmans.

Fanny Bullock Workman and her husband William Hunter Workman were an American mountaineering-team, of which Fanny was very much the dominant partner. The Workmans were rich, energetic and adventurous. They arrived in India in 1898, and immediately bicycled from Cape Comorin in the south to the Himalayas in the north. They then spent the next twelve years in the Himalayas, Karakoram and Hindu Kush, exploring and climbing mountains which in those days were virtually unknown.

The Workmans were controversial figures. British writers have usually played down their achievements, pointing out that their maps were sometimes inaccurate, that their claims were often exaggerated, and that their relationship with their porters was always abysmal. Certainly the last of these criticisms is justified. The Workmans treated their porters like dirt. "I have never known their equal," writes the outraged Fanny, "for shirking work, deserting, demanding double rations, looting and mutinying." She goes on to describe what she calls a "mutiny". *"We began a zig-zag up the slope which in places had a gradient of 60°.*

Above: William and Fanny Bullock Workman, an adventurous mountaineering team.
Right and opposite: The indomitable Fanny faces the perils of river and crevasse.

The snow had become softened by the heat of the sun, and our guide was kept busy treading out steps to help the advance of the coolies (native porters). But when the coolies arrived at the base of the slope, they all sat down, and their leader called up weakly that they were tired and could go no farther. We answered, 'Tell them they must' . . . At this, they started up the slope; but after a short distance they again stopped in a determined manner, and nothing could persuade them to move . . . Our guide did his best to explain matters to them, but they only became more excited. Suddenly three of them attacked the guide. He, in self-defence, struck the strongest of them over the back with his ice-axe, felling him to the ground. That settled the issue. That argument they understood. They fell into line, and began to file slowly upward." A sad little story, which

was to be repeated many times on many peaks. The Workmans didn't love their fellow human beings.

They did, however, love the mountains. And between 1899 and 1912 they returned to them again and again: exploring, discovering, surveying and above all climbing, with an enthusiasm never seen before and seldom since. Fanny, indeed, climbed higher than any woman had ever climbed – and very nearly as high as any man – an achievement all the more remarkable since she was getting on for fifty years old. Now it is true that the Workmans were not in some respects, very attractive characters. It is true that some of the mountains they claimed to have discovered were in fact first sighted by somebody else; and it is true that some of the heights they claimed to have reached were exaggerated. But what saves them, what shines through each and every one of their expedition-reports, is their enthusiasm. The mountains' difficulties and dangers they made light of. The mountains' beauties and splendours never failed to excite them.

On their first expedition (1899) they explored the Hispar-Biafo Glacier in the Karakoram climbing a peak of over 6,000 metres, the Koser Gunge. Fanny disappeared up to her neck in the soft snow, was dragged headfirst through a glacier stream, and left dangling over a bottomless crevasse. Here is her account of the last of these near-disasters. *"An occasion which I found trying was on a mild morning after a heavy fall of snow. Our guide had just crossed a snow-bridge spanning a crevasse. He called to me to step lightly. But, alas, too late; for the bridge collapsed, taking me with it. We were roped; and the guide on the one side and those on the rope on the other side withstood the strain. It was not, however, a pleasant sensation to find my arms and neck embedded in soft clinging snow, and the rest of my body swinging about in space. 'Push out your feet, and pull yourself up,' shouted the guide. 'Very good,' I replied. 'But with a void beneath me, there is nothing to push on!' However, by baring my hands of both gloves and skin, and by strenuous hauling on the rope, I at last made a successful if not triumphant exit."* A few days later the Workmans were camped at 5,015 metres (higher than the top of Mont Blanc) *"enjoying the most glorious view. Although we were shivering with cold and longing for hot tea, we rejoiced in our lonely but magnificent bivouac, and would not have exchanged it at any price for the warmth and comfort of a Swiss hut."*

A couple of years later the Workmans were once again in the Karakoram, drawn back to the great peaks as iron is drawn to a magnet.

41

The Bullock Workmans' long-suffering porters.

The highlight of their second expedition was Fanny's ascent of Watershed Peak (6,512m). This involved a climb of some technical difficulty and considerable danger. Fanny had to swing herself round a pinnacle on two sides of which there was a sheer drop of more than 1,200 metres. "Don't look, madam, at the precipices," said their guide laconically. "Just swing round quickly!" Once she fell; her feet shot from under her, and she was only saved from certain death by her rope. But the view from the summit made it all worthwhile. *"It was,"* she wrote, *"the most beautiful I have ever seen. For the single pyramid of Watershed Peak stands alone, with no near higher summits to mar the view. Six thousand feet (2,000 metres) beneath us lay Snow Lake, its glacial branches spread out like white fans. Beyond, the peak Kailasa rose like a great medieval castle in turrets of ice and snow. Far*

away, apparently suspended between earth and sky, hung the grey massif of K2. Watershed Peak offered us from its summit a panorama of one of the most magnificent mountain-landscapes in the world. I felt I had seen wonders, the memory of which will cling while life lasts."

The Workmans' final expedition was their greatest. In 1912 they explored the remote Siachan (Rose) Glacier in the east Karakoram. Twelve years in the mountains had mellowed the Workmans a little – a little, but not much! One incident near the head of the glacier spotlights both their continuing intolerance of their porters and their abiding love of the mountains. Fanny tells us that the meaning of Siachan is "rose-bush", and that the glacier got its name from the "great profusion of wild roses, which flourish in pink splendour right up to the foot of the moraine". She then goes on to say that she herself has another explanation of the name. *"We were,"* she writes, *"camped on* the glacier in tempestuous weather, waiting to recross the pass. I had been kept awake late by great gusts of wind, and, more particularly, by the loud dirge-like chanting of the coolies which rose irritatingly above the howling of the wind. Exasperated, I threw on a coat and went out to make them stop their coolie-noise. It was still snowing on the glacier, but above the peak of Tarim Shehr the clouds had parted, and a full moon shone with splendour upon an exquisite scene. As I stood there, I suddenly realized that all about me the undulating hillocks of ice were covered with large, feathery, full-blown snow-roses. It was not an hallucination. The roses were perfectly formed out of snow. I buried my hands in their cold, silvery petals, and forgetting the zero temperature, stood chained by the poetry of my surroundings. The great peak, moon-bathed from base to summit, looked down upon the rose-hills; the chant of the coolies rose stridently and yet in harmony with the roar of the wind, and the moon, hung in a black sky, cast its resplendent light over all."

It is good to record that Fanny was so impressed with what she calls the "weird glory" of the scene, that she went back to her tent without stopping the chant of her "coolies".

There have been greater mountaineers than Fanny Bullock Workman, but none more enthusiastic. She loved the mountains; and for that much can be forgiven her.

Gasherbrum II, one of the great peaks in the Karakoram, first climbed by an Austrian expedition in 1956.

5 Through the Eight-Thousand Metre Barrier

Maurice Herzog, leader of the French Himalayan expedition, who in 1950 climbed the first 8,000 metre peak – Annapurna I (8091m).

Time and again during the first half of the 20th century mountaineers attempted to climb the great peaks of the Himalayas and the Karakoram. Time and again they failed. Right up to 1950 nobody had ever climbed one of the *really* major peaks: i.e. a peak of over 8,000 metres. It was as though 8,000 metres was a barrier beyond which mankind was unable to ascend. Then a French expedition, led by Maurice Herzog, arrived at the foot of Annapurna.

It seemed unlikely that the French would succeed where all other nations had failed; for Herzog and his team had virtually no experience of climbing in the Himalayas, and the peaks they had decided to attempt were little-known and looked impossibly difficult. The French climbers did, however, have one advantage over their predecessors. They were able to approach the mountains from the south. For more than a hundred years Nepal had banned Europeans from its territory. Mountaineering expeditions had therefore been obliged to tackle the Himalayas *via* their north-facing slopes, from Tibet. It was not until 1949 that Nepal lifted its ban; and the first people to take advantage of the new approach this offered were the French.

Herzog's expedition was organised by the French Alpine Club, whose president spelt out very clearly both their objectives and the difficulties they would have to face. *"Many expeditions of many nationalities have tried to climb an 8,000-metre peak. None has succeeded. You will attempt either Dhaulagiri (8,167m) or Annapurna (8,091m) . . . Up to now Himalayan expeditions have picked objectives in regions already known and explored. We know virtually nothing about our 'eight-thousanders'. The approaches to them are un-* trodden by Europeans; the maps of their upper regions are inaccurate. You will therefore have to do a great deal of reconnaissance before you can launch an assault."* It all sounded, as Herzog put it, "a tremendous challenge".

The French expedition's first glimpse of the Himalayas was spectacular: a huge wall of ice and rock rising near-sheer from the plains. *"To start with,"* wrote Herzog, *"we saw nothing but mist. Then, looking more closely, we could make out in the distance a terrific wall of ice rising above the mist to an unbelievable height, and blocking the entire northern horizon for hundreds of miles. We were quite over-*

whelmed by its magnificence and grandeur." The first glimpse of the peaks they hoped to climb was even more spectacular. *"We were woken by a shout from Noyelle: 'Look! Dhaulagiri!' Everyone was out in a flash, covering his nakedness with whatever came to hand – in Lachenal's case his ski cap! An enormous ice-pyramid, glittering in the sun like crystal, soared up more than 23,000 feet (7,000 metres) immediately above us. Its southern face, shining blue through the rising mist was unbelievably lofty; not of this world. The sight was magnificent; but from a mountaineering point of view disappointing, for we could see there was not the slightest hope of an ascent via the south face."*

The peaks of Dhaulagiri and Annapurna lie side by side, separated only by the narrow slit of the Kali Gandaki gorge, probably the most spectacular valley on Earth. The two mountains may be neighbours but they are very different. Dhaulagiri is a single, steep-sided pyramid. Annapurna is a long, complex ridge with many summits, the highest of which (Annapurna I) cannot be seen from the south.

Herzog and his team decided to tackle Dhaulagiri first. They made three determined reconnaissance climbs, only to be thwarted on each occasion by stupendous walls of rock and ice and by the mountain's sheer size – "Everything," Herzog admitted, "is *far* larger than we anticipated". These reconnaissance climbs occupied the better part of a month. It was mid-May before Herzog turned his attention to Annapurna. By this time his chance of conquering an "eight-thousander" seemed, to say the least, remote. For he hadn't yet even located the summit of Annapurna, and already the brief climbing-season was drawing to a close. (This season lasts only from approximately April 1st when the winter snows have thawed, to approximately June 1st when the monsoon rain-clouds come sweeping in from the Bay of Bengal.) To find *and* climb an 8,000-metre peak in little more than a fortnight seemed out of the question. But Herzog was determined to try.

The French climbers all agreed that the south face of Annapurna looked "impossible". They had therefore to attempt the north face.

The only possible route to the north face lay *via* the Miristi Khola gorge, a branch of the Kali Gandaki which was marked on their maps as "impenetrable". Herzog and his team proved the maps were wrong. After nearly a week of forcing their way through little-used forest tracks, they emerged into the north Annapurna basin, "a savage and desolate cirque of mountains never before seen by man". The weather was bad, with low cloud and heavy falls of snow. However, at dawn on May 23rd the climbers woke to find that the sky had miraculously cleared. *"Now for the first time,"* wrote Herzog, *"Annapurna was revealing its secrets. The huge north face, with its great rivers of ice lay before us, sparkling in the sunlight. Never had I seen so impressive a mountain. It was a world both dazzling and menacing; the eye was lost in its immensities. But for once we were not confronted with vertical walls and hanging glaciers which put an end to all thoughts of climbing. Lachenal was pointing: 'If only we could get to the foot of that sickle-shaped glacier' . . ."*

That afternoon they radioed the Alpine Club in Paris: *"Have decided to attempt the summit via North Annapurna Glacier. Route entirely snow and ice. Weather favourable. Have high hopes."* Within the hour four climbers – Herzog, Lachenal, Rébuffat and Terray – were heading up the mountain. The reconnaissance had become an assault.

Herzog realised that with the monsoon due in a matter of days rather than weeks, they had no time to lay siege to Annapurna by traditional methods. Their only hope was to make a dash for the summit, hoping and praying that behind them their companions and Sherpas would be able to set up camps to which they could fall back in an emergency.

In the week between May 24th and June 1st the four climbers hauled themselves up from a little over 4,000 metres to a little over 7,000 metres. The climb was dangerous. At one place they had to cross an ice-gully down which avalanches were "crashing almost continuously with a hideous din". It was also difficult. On one ice-wall it took them all their strength and all their expertise to climb six metres in an hour. However, by June 2nd

Herzog and Lachenal had managed to pitch their tent half-way up the great arête which sweeps up to Annapurna's summit. And, what was equally important, their Sherpas had managed to set up a series of camps below them.

The position of Herzog's and Lachenal's tent on the night of June 2nd was terrifying. There was no level ground and no shelter. All they could do was hack out a tiny ledge on the exposed slope. Above them, spindrift hissing down from the summit piled up against the upper wall of their tent, threatening to dislodge it. Below them a precipice fell sheer for more than a thousand metres into the North Annapurna Basin. To quote Herzog. *"It was a grim night. Our minds worked slowly. We hadn't the energy to cook a meal. It was all we could do to make some tea and force ourselves to swallow our pills. After dark a fierce wind sprang up, making the tent flap and quiver. At each gust we clung in terror to the tent-pole as drowning men to a straw. We slept little. I was on the upper side of the tent, and spent the night convinced that I was being suffocated by the snow which piled up, ever heavier and deeper, against the canvas. Lachenal, on the lower side, spent the night convinced that any moment we were about to be swept over the precipice."* At dawn they were again too weak to cook a meal. They struggled into their boots, swallowed a handful of Maxiton tablets, and set out, unroped, for the summit. Maxiton is an effective short-term stimulant; but if too many tablets are taken on an empty stomach they bring about an uncaring euphoria. This may explain much of what happened next.

All morning Herzog and Lachenal struggled up the arête. The climbing was not technically difficult. It was, however, almost unbearably exhausting. In the thin air they found it hard to breathe. They took one step forward, then had to stop, panting and gasping, before they could take the next. By mid-day they were both badly frostbitten, and suffering from hallucinations. *"It was,"* wrote Herzog, *"as though I was standing outside myself, and watching our paltry efforts from another world. There was no gravity. The landscape was diaphanous. This wasn't the mountain I knew on which I was standing; it was the mountain of my dreams."*

Then, suddenly, they were on the summit. A fierce wind was tearing into them. On all sides Annapurna fell away: to the south so sharply that they felt if they took just one step forward they would fall sheer to the plains beneath. But what a moment of triumph it was! For the first time in history human beings had climbed a mountain of over 8,000 metres.

Their troubles, however, were not over. Indeed they had barely begun. Herzog wanted to stay awhile on the summit, taking photographs. Lachenal, anxious about his frostbitten feet, wanted to descend at once. Incredibly, they parted company. On the way back to their tent, the two climbers became enveloped in cloud, and lost sight of one another. Herzog lost his gloves; it wasn't long before his hands were as badly frostbitten as his feet. Lachenal fell; he lost his ice-axe, his balaclava and one of his crampons. If their companions, Rébuffat and Terray, hadn't climbed up to help them, Herzog and Lachenal would probably have died on the arête. As it was, the four of them spent a terrible night in their tent, with Rébuffat and Terray trying desperately to massage life into their companions' limbs which were "white and solid as marble", while outside the wind howled and the snow fell as Annapurna was swept by a full-scale blizzard.

Next morning there was a white-out. The snow was so thick they couldn't see from one end of their rope to the other. They knew, however, it was no good staying in their tent: that their only hope of saving Herzog's and Lachenal's lives was to get down as fast as they could to the doctor, some 1,500 metres below in Camp II. By this time Lachenal's feet were so swollen that he couldn't get them into his boots. The unselfish Terray gave him his. And the four of them set out into the blizzard, half-lame and half-snowblind, hoping to reach Camp IV before dark.

They had a difficult and dangerous descent, sinking up to their waists in the soft, new-fallen snow; and the farther they descended the worse conditions became. The snow deepened. The light faded. The temperature dropped; and as night approached, their expectation of life grew less with every passing minute. Suddenly Lachenal gave a cry of

The Annapurna ridge, from Nepal.

fear, and disappeared. He had fallen into a crevasse. Although at the time it seemed like the last straw, the crevasse in fact saved their lives. For it turned out to be no more than 5 metres deep: a natural cave of ice in which they were able to shelter for the night. But once again what a night it was! Even more harrowing than the one before, as they huddled together, trying to massage warmth into one another's frozen limbs. By dawn they were so weak that Herzog, as he was lifted out of the ice-cave, thought he was dying; he begged the others to go on without him. The others, however, were in no condition to go anywhere. For they found to their horror that they were snow-blind.

Again the expectation of life – but never the will to live – ebbed out of them. Mercifully, the weather had now cleared. So, with the blind and the maimed helping one another as best they could, they struggled into their boots and started shouting for help. They had very nearly lost hope, when, as if by a miracle, a figure

appeared waist-deep in snow, "ploughing his way towards (them) like a boat through heavy seas". Their companions from Camp IV had found them.

The four climbers had been reprieved; but they hadn't been saved. For they still had to descend more than 1,000 metres to reach the doctor and the comparative safety of Camp II. They set off at once: knowing that the newly-fallen snow was likely to avalanche, but knowing too that Herzog and Lachenal would die if they weren't given medical attention. For the injured men the descent was a nightmare. The blind had to be led. The injured had to be half-supported, half-carried. As Herzog tried to lower himself by ropes over an ice-fall, the skin was torn in great strips from his injured hands. Then they were hit by an avalanche. *"An elemental force,"* writes Herzog, *"flung me head over heels. Snow enveloped me, making it impossible to breathe. I was spun round and round like a puppet. As in a kaleidoscope, I saw flashes of brilliant sunlight through the snow that was pouring past my eyes. The rope joining me to the Sherpas coiled round my neck. Again and again I crashed into solid ice as the avalanche swept me down through the seracs. Suddenly the rope tightened, and I was brought to a halt, dangling upside down in a chimney of blue ice. In an uncontrollable spasm I passed water, and lost consciousness."* Herzog and two of the Sherpas had come to rest suspended by the same rope, on either side of a serac (ice pinnacle): a serac which was no more than a couple of hundred metres from the lip of a precipice. Another few seconds and they would have been swept to certain death. As it was, they were dug out, shocked but not seriously injured. "At least," as Herzog put it, "we had made the descent to Camp II in record time!"

That night rescued and rescuers alike crowded together into the little cluster of tents at the side of the North Annapurna Glacier. The battle to climb the world's first 8,000-metre peak had been won. The battle to save Herzog's and Lachenal's lives had still to be decided.

Both climbers were in bad shape. To quote Herzog: *"My limbs were completely numb beyond the ankles and wrists. There was practically no skin on my hands, and what little there was hung down in long black strips; my fingers were swollen and grotesquely distorted. My feet were brown and violet, without feeling. In my arms and legs the blood-pressure was virtually nil. My blood was thick, clotted and black as a black pudding."* Their doctor, Jacques Oudot, worked tirelessly to save them. He gave them dressings, massage and intravenous injections – the latter so agonising that they caused convulsions and delirium.

On June 6th Camp II was evacuated. The monsoon by now had broken in earnest. Snow and sleet fell without respite, and the rivers were in flood. Travelling for men who were fit would have been difficult. For men who were half-blind and wholly crippled, it was another nightmare. That they got back at all was due to their Sherpas, who took it in turns to carry the injured climbers over some of the most difficult terrain in the Himalayas. At last the expedition struggled through to the comparative safety of the Kali Gandaki; but not before every one of

Lachenal's toes, as they turned gangrenous, had to be amputated one by one. Herzog was even more unfortunate. He lost all his toes *and* all his fingers.

Annapurna had been conquered. But at a terrible price.

The climbing of Annapurna was like the opening of a sluice-gate. It precipitated a flood: a flood of successful climbs. Before the ascent of Annapurna not a single major peak had been climbed. Within five years of the ascent of Annapurna almost every major peak had been climbed – including Everest.

The climbing of Everest was a triumph for the Royal Geographical Society. The links between the Society and the highest mountain in the world were first forged in 1919, when the then president of the Society, Francis Young-husband, decided to form a special Himalayan Committee whose task would be to master-mind a British ascent. Throughout the 1920s and 30s the Himalayan Committee planned, and the Society sponsored, a whole series of expeditions to Everest. All failed; although in 1924 Mallory and Irvine came tantalisingly close to success. After World War II, the Committee reconsidered its task in the light of two new developments. Everest could now be approached from the south; and the use of oxygen had become both practical and acceptable. In 1951 a reconnaissance expedition led by Eric Shipton was sent to explore the southern approaches to Everest, with instructions to try and find a mysterious valley known as the Western Cwm which was believed to nestle between the slopes of Everest and the neighbouring peak of Lhotse.

Shipton's expedition was successful. And what an exciting moment it must have been for Shipton and Hillary when they first sighted the Western Cwm and the possible route that this mysterious valley provided to the summit. *"At 19,000 feet (5,800 metres),"* writes Hillary, *"we stopped for a rest and admired the wonderful views that were opening up around us. Almost casually I looked towards the Western Cwm, although I didn't expect to see much of it from here. To my astonishment the whole valley lay revealed to our eyes. A long, narrow, snowy trough swept from the top of the ice-fall and*

Two great mountaineers. (Left) Eric Shipton, (Right) John Hunt.

climbed steeply up the face of Lhotse to the head of the Cwm. And even as the same thought was simmering in my own mind, Shipton said 'There's a route there!' And I could hear the disbelief in his voice . . . In excited voices we discussed our find. We had neither the equipment nor the men to take advantage of our discovery, but at least we could try and find a route up the ice-fall, and then return next year and attack the mountain in force."

It was in fact 1953 before the British returned to Everest, this time with a large team of climbers and porters led by John Hunt. Hunt's expedition succeeded in climbing Everest whereas all previous expeditions had failed partly because Shipton had pioneered a practicable route for them, partly because they used oxygen on an unprecedented scale, and partly because Hunt turned out to be an inspired leader.

Shipton's new route certainly didn't provide an easy way up the mountain – there was no such thing! It did, however, have several advantages over all the routes which had been tried before. In particular, it lay up the south side of the mountain, rather than the north. The north face of Everest may *look* relatively easy, but from a climber's point of view it has serious drawbacks. Its upper reaches are exposed to the full force of the northwest gales which lash the summit on four days out of five. The northerly tilt of the rock-strata means there are few footholds and even fewer level ledges on which to pitch a tent. The lack of sun means that it isn't possible to make an early start to the day's climbing. Above all, the most difficult climbing occurs in the last 450 metres, at a height at which climbers are least able to cope with difficulties. The south face of Everest may *look* impossible – stupendous cliffs and sheer, beautifully-fluted walls of ice – but the Western Cwm provides a flaw in these defences. Also the most difficult climbing occurs at a comparatively low altitude, in the ice-fall. Shipton, in 1951, had already pioneered a route up the ice-fall; and where he had led, Hunt and his team felt confident they could follow.

Above: The Western Cwm, key to the ascent of Everest.
Right: Hillary and Tenzing on their way to the summit.

The British team's use of oxygen was every bit as important as its choice of route. Indeed, to quote the then president of the Royal Geographical Society, *"the use of oxygen was the secret of success . . . This expedition,"* the president wrote, *"differed in one vital respect from those of previous years. The intention of the earlier expeditions had always been to try and reach the summit without the use of oxygen, and if this should prove impossible, to turn to oxygen only when absolutely necessary. As a result no climbers above 26,000 feet (8,000*

Nanga Parbat, "The killer mountain", responsible for more climbers' deaths than any other peak in the Himalayas.

metres) *were in prime physical condition. The Himalayan Committee took the view that oxygen was needed on a much bigger scale than formerly, that it was in fact the secret of success. This large-scale use of oxygen necessitated a heavy lift for the porters; and the amount of oxygen which had to be carried decided the size of the expedition. A small expedition was out of the question; a large expedition was essential . . . Hunt's plan was that all climbers should become accustomed to the use of oxygen during the training climbs, that oxygen should be used while sleeping, and that oxygen should be used for all climbing above the South Col. This plan was adhered to."* As a result, the British were able to establish half-a-dozen fit climbers no more than 600 metres below the summit.

But no matter how well-chosen the British expedition's route and no matter how beneficial their oxygen, these factors alone would not have brought about success. The success of *any* expedition depends on the strength and cohesion of its members, and this in turn depends very largely on its leadership. Hunt was a splendid leader. Almost every book about Everest points out that he was a colonel in the Army, and that he "planned the ascent of Everest like a military campaign, with meticulous attention to detail." It is not so often pointed out that Hunt was not only a strong and efficient leader, he was also a kind and understanding one, who showed great skill in welding the individual members of his expedition into a happy and united team. "What a very *happy* party you've got going," one of his climbers said to him on their way to the base camp. The British team who first climbed Everest deserve to be remembered not only for their success, but also for their sense of comradeship and their love of the mountains. It is worth thinking about that Hunt refused to call his book "The *Conquest* of Everest," preferring instead the gentler word "ascent"; also that his climbers took with them to the top of the world not only a British flag but a crucifix.

6 The Himalayas Today

Until recently almost the only people to set eyes on the Himalayas – apart from those lucky enough to live there – were the mountaineers of big expeditions. Today this has changed; and the Himalayas are now visited each year by countless small groups of mountaineers and scientists, and by tens of thousands of trekkers.

It might have been thought that when Mount Everest and the other major peaks had been climbed, mountaineers would be left, like Alexander the Great, "sighing for new worlds to conquer." This didn't happen. For the mountaineers brought to the great peaks of Asia a new and more exciting way of climbing.

In the old days the high peaks of the Himalayas were nearly always attempted by what was known as the siege method. This involved big expeditions, with relays of porters carrying tons of supplies to the base of a mountain. Climbers and porters would then methodically set up a succession of camps – sometimes as many as a dozen – on their way to the summit; each camp would be stockpiled with food and equipment before the next was established. All this involved weeks, if not months, of climbing, with members of the expedition constantly ascending and descending the mountain. There was nothing wrong with this type of climbing; but it did call for a lot of time, a lot of people, a lot of money and a lot of organisation. Some climbers felt that this took the fun out of mountaineering, and that a lower-key and more individual approach would be more satisfying. There had always been champions of this lower-key approach; most of Eric Shipton's famous climbs, for example, were made with small light-weight teams of only three or four people. And after the ascent of Everest this type of small expedition came into its own. For as soon as big expeditions had climbed the major peaks *via* their easiest routes, small expeditions began to attempt them *via* their more difficult routes. This involved a change from the siege method of climbing to the Alpine method.

The challenges which await climbers in the Himalayas. Below: bridging a crevasse. Right: climbing an ice wall.

The essence of the Alpine method is that a *small* number of climbers attempt the summit in a *quick* push. They set off from the bottom of a mountain carrying all their equipment and food, and make a continuous and self-contained advance. So a peak which would have taken many weeks to climb by the old method was now attempted in a few days. The dangers are obvious. The mountaineers have to be fully acclimatized before they start, or they will fail at high altitude; in the case of injury or exhaustion they have no companions to help them; in the case of bad weather they have no well-stocked camps to fall back on. Not only their success but their very lives depend on their speed, stamina and sound judgement. This Alpine method has been aptly described by Chris Bonington as "the most challenging but also the most satisfying form of mountaineering".

In the 1970's and 80's many mountaineers from many countries came to the Himalayas to climb by this Alpine method. Technically these modern mountaineers are often more skilful than their predecessors. Their equipment is also better. The result is that they have made some remarkable climbs which would have been considered impossible twenty or thirty years ago. Herzog, for example, wrote of Dhaulagiri, "I doubt if it will *ever* be climbed;" today Dhaulagiri has been climbed half a dozen times. For years Everest withstood the challenge of the mountaineering *élite* of the world; today Everest has been climbed by half a dozen routes, it has been climbed by women, it has been climbed without oxygen, and it has been climbed solo.

British climbers like Chris Bonington, Doug Scott, Peter Boardman and Joe Tasker have been particularly active in pioneering this Alpine method of climbing. If asked which was the most important of their exploits, I would vote for Bonington's ascent of Kongur.

Kongur was important for several reasons. In 1980 the Chinese, for the first time in years, agreed to allow foreign expeditions to go climbing in the Pamir and Kun Lun. First into this little-known area was the British Mount Kongur Expedition; and it was obviously important to establish from the start a good relationship with the Chinese. Equally import-

ant was the medical research into high altitude sickness carried out by the expedition leader, Dr. Michael Ward, who was a lecturer and surgeon at the University of London. Millions of people now trek to high altitudes each year. Many suffer from oedema (a build-up of fluid in the brain and lungs), and from eye-haemorrhage (bleeding). Research in this field was therefore of practical value to a lot of people. Finally, from the mountaineering point of view, Kongur (7,719m) was one of the last major unclimbed peaks in the world; and the expedition hoped to climb it by the Alpine method. What a challenge!

Kongur lies in a remote region of the Chinese Pamir, close to the Soviet border. It is a giant of a mountain, with a summit-pyramid of considerable technical difficulty. Much of the time it is hidden by cloud, and lashed by violent storms. If there *was* a route to its summit, no-one had yet found it. Reconnaissance was therefore essential, and in the summer of 1980 an advance party consisting of Bonington,

Michael Ward, leader of the Mount Kongur Expedition, looking towards the peaks his team were the first to climb.

Rouse and Ward approached the mountain *via* Lake Karakul. This was Kirghiz country: the terrain vast and desolate with its horizons pushed back to the very rim of the world, the people nomadic and hospitable and still clinging to their traditional way of life. *"They live as they have done for centuries,"* writes Ward, *"herding their flocks. To control these they ride small, hardy horses; man and horse are welded together and move as one. The women wore jewelry around their necks similar to that seen in the sketches of 19th century travel books."* The reconnaissance party soon found that the closer they came to Kongur, the less they were able to form an overall picture of the mountain. *"Sudden fierce winds with snow, sleet and rain came out of a cloudless sky; and over the Kongur Massif clouds constantly formed and vanished, blotting out the details of this complex range."* They therefore decided to try and climb a peak some way to the south of Kongur, and to

look for a route from there. They managed to climb Sarakyaguqi (6,200m), and from its summit were able at last to see the whole enormous southwest face of Kongur, and what looked like a possible route to the summit-pyramid *via* the Koksel Glacier. Soon they were reconnoitring this glacier, and in particular a narrow corridor up it, only just over a metre wide: a corridor which was swept almost continuously by stones and avalanches. This turned out to be the only route to the summit!

A year later the main expedition, again led by Ward and with a climbing team of Bonington, Boardman, Rouse and Tasker, was back at the foot of the mountain. They set up their base camp in a flower-covered meadow at the foot of the glacial moraine, "an idyllic spot". As soon as the four climbers were acclimatised, they set off for the summit.

The very essence of the Alpine method is speed. But speed on Kongur was easier to aim at than to achieve; for the mountain was technically difficult and the weather appalling. The climbers managed, in three days, to struggle up to the summit ridge (7,350m). Here they were brought up short by bad visibility and worsening weather. During the night of June 25th the wind rose to such fury that the four men slept fully clothed, expecting their tents any moment to be ripped away. Next morning, through driving spindrift, they had their first close sight of the summit-pyramid, and were appalled. It looked impossible: a sheer ice-coated mountain piled on top of the mountain they had already climbed. They dug out a snow-cave, and waited for the weather to clear. When it did clear – briefly – they began to work their way towards the summit-pyramid along a knife-edged ridge of ice overhung by unstable pinnacles of rock. In six hours they managed to climb no more than 100 metres. With their food almost exhausted and the weather again worsening, it was obvious the summit was beyond them. They retreated, very prudently, to the foot of the Koksel Glacier.

A week later they tried again, leaving be-

hind their tents so that they could carry more food. This was a gamble, with their lives as the stakes. The four climbers again managed to reach the main ridge without too much difficulty; and here they spent the night of July 6th in the snow cave which they had hollowed out during their first attempt. Next day they managed to traverse the difficult knife-edge ridge which led to the foot of the final pyramid. They hoped to spend the night beneath the pyramid

Animals at work.
Right: Yak and cart.
Below: a well-laden train of camels.

in a snow cave; but much to their disappoint-
ment, found that the snow was no more than a
thin layer on top of hard ice. All they could do
was hack-out four shallow and narrow de-
pressions, like coffins. In these "coffins" they
spent the next four days, clinging precariously
to the roof of the world, while violent storms
lashed the summit. Many times their "coffins"
had to be rebuilt – Al Rouse's collapsed on top
of him; their sleeping bags grew wetter and
colder; their food supplies dwindled; their
hopes sank. However, on July 12th the snow
eased off, and although it was still bitterly cold
and blowing a gale, the four men set out to
attempt the final pyramid. The first 150 metres
were technically difficult: sheer as the face of
the Eiger; in some places ice, in other places
brittle, crumbling rock. It was 2 p.m. before
they reached the top of the rock-band, and
8 p.m. before, at last, they stood triumphant on
the summit. Here they were buffeted by
hammer blows of wind, and a maelstrom of
spindrift. Above and around them the sky was
a deep dark blue, brilliantly clear. Below them
cotton-wool clouds stretched from horizon to
horizon, hiding the surrounding peaks. They
photographed one another, holding the British,
Chinese and expedition flags, conscious all the

time of the danger of frostbite and exposure:
conscious too of the fact that they were going to
have to sleep that night, without tents, at a
height of something like 7,700 metres. They
spent only a few minutes on the summit, then
descended about 30 metres to a snow slope
where they laboriously dug out a cave.

They slept surprisingly well, the highest
men in the world, and were woken next morning by the sun pouring in through the entrance
of their snow-cave. It was a perfect day. They
returned to the top of Kongur, and spent some
hours climbing a subsidiary summit, just to be
certain that they had indeed set foot on the
highest point. There was only one other com-
mitment now that they had to honour. On the
top of the mountain, not far from the spot where
a century earlier Holdich had written that "the
British, Russian and Chinese empires came
together", they buried a prayer for the peace
of the world. A couple of days later they were
back at the foot of the Koksel Glacier, drinking
not only to their successful ascent, but to continuing friendship with their Chinese hosts.
The expedition, in every way, had been a
success.

The Koksel Basin, Mount Kongur.

In the celebrations that followed the ascent of Kongur, Ward and his team drank to the health of their hosts the Chinese Mountaineering Association, the health of their sponsors Jardine Matheson, and the health of the organisation who had worked untiringly for more than ten years to bring their expedition to fruition, the Mount Everest Foundation.

No organisation has done more in recent years to advance the cause of British and New Zealand mountaineering than the Everest Foundation. It came into being in 1953, its purpose being to manage the surplus funds which accrued from the first ascent of Everest. It was – and still is – run by a Management Committee drawn from members of the Royal Geographical Society and the Alpine Club; and in the last thirty-odd years it has supported no fewer than 700 mountaineering expeditions, and has given away nearly £400,000 in grants. It was responsible for the first ascents of Kangchenjunga, Nuptse, the South Face of Annapurna, The Ogre and Kongur. It has also been responsible for expeditions carrying out research in the mountains in such far-away places as the Patagonian Ice Camp (Chile), Rwanda (central Africa), Antarctica and New Guinea. In 1980 it was one of several organisations who helped to sponsor an International expedition to the Karakoram.

The International Karakoram Project was typical of the new type of expedition which in recent years has replaced the old exploring type. It is not enough nowadays for an explorer to find a mountain and a mountaineer to climb it. Both want to know all about that mountain, and in particular how it affects the lives of those who live in its shadow. It was to answer these questions that the members of the International Karakoram Project assembled in 1980 in the Hunza Valley.

The Hunza Valley lies in one of the remotest inhabited areas on Earth, the complex knot of mountains where the Himalayas, the Hindu Kush and the Karakoram come together in a

The flowers of the Himalayas attract both botanists and tourists. Among the most beautiful are: (Top) Rhododendron. (Centre) Magnolia. (Bottom) Primulas.

jumble of high peaks and deep valleys. This is a world of spectacular contrasts: the beauty of the small well-cultivated terraces contrasting with the vast slopes of arid rock, and the vast slopes of arid rock contrasting with the snowy grandeur of the peaks. It is a world in transition. For beneath the Earth's surface the continental plate of India is boring into the the continental plate of central Aisa, and this collision of the plates triggers off a near-continuous succession of earthquakes, earth-tremors, landslides, avalanches and floods. Nowhere else in the world is one so conscious so often of the elemental forces that are still fashioning our planet. It was primarily to measure these forces that some sixty scientists – most of them surveyors, geologists, geomorphologists or seismologists – came to the Hunza. Two aspects of their work were of particular importance: their pinpoint surveying, and their efforts to see that their studies brought benefit to the local population.

The Hunza Valley had been last surveyed in 1913 by Kenneth Mason. Mason had written: *"The country is extremely difficult. We relied on observing light-signals, which meant leaving men on the mountain tops perhaps for a week on end, ready to show a lamp-flash by night or a helio-flash by day. The average height of our stations was about 17,500 feet (5,300m)."* In spite of these difficulties, Mason managed to complete a survey of meticulous accuracy, his heights and positions of the great peaks often being exact to within centimetres. During the planning of the International Karakoram Project it was realised that the accuracy of Mason's survey could provide the basis for an intriguing study . . . If the scientists of the Project could survey the Hunza with the same accuracy as Mason, then, by comparing the positions of 1980 with the positions of 1913, it would be possible to see how far the peaks had moved in the intervening years; this in turn would show how fast the plate of India was boring into the plate of central Asia. In their determination to match Mason for accuracy, the surveyors of the International Karakoram Project pushed themselves to the utmost. One of them, Jim Bishop, fell to his death setting up an observation post on the summit of Kurkun (4,730m). But in spite of the difficulties and dangers, triangulation was carried out over a wide area with unprecedented precision. When comparisons were made, it was found that many of the peaks had moved by as much as six metres in the 67 years between 1913 and 1980. India, in other words, is still boring into central Asia at a rate of something like 80mm a year. In scientific terms this was an important discovery.

In human terms some of the Project's work was of equal importance. Its "housing and natural hazards group", for example, carried out surveys on the health of the village people and the strength of the village houses. It is true that their findings were neither conclusive nor dramatic; but the fact that this sort of research was being carried out at all was, in itself, significant. For it indicated recognition of the fact that the work of expeditions should be related to the needs of the local people, that knowledge only becomes of value when it is used to enhance the quality of people's lives. So, in their very different ways, the scientists who worked in the Hunza and the mountaineers who climbed on Kongur were both successful.

These two expeditions are typical of the Alpine-style climbs and the research-orientated projects which are now opening up the Himalayas to the rest of the world. And how dramatically, in recent years, the number of these expeditions has increased. In the mid 1960s there were less than ten expeditions a year to the Himalayas; today there are over two-hundred.

Even more dramatic has been the increase in the number of tourists, and, in particular, trekkers. In the mid 1960s no more than 100 trekkers ventured each year into the mountains. Today the figure has risen to close on 100,000! There are package tours up the Kali Gandaki Gorge; a luxury hotel nestles close to the foot of Everest. It is good news that the most magnificent mountains on Earth can now be seen and appreciated by large numbers of ordinary people. However, the opening up of the mountains has led to problems and dangers; and with the privilege of visiting the Himalayas has come the obligation to care for and protect them.

One might have thought that so vast and awesome a region as the mountains of central Asia would need no protection, that the greatest ranges on Earth would be well able to look after themselves. However, 20th century man has a huge capacity for destruction, and the ecology of the mountains is more fragile than appears at first sight. To give just a few examples of the hazards now facing the region . . . Today's tourist route to Everest has been described as "a garbage trail, full of tins, bottles and junk". The Rongbuk Monastery now lies in ruins, "filled with thousands of tins, boxes, paper and decaying food." Even the South Col of Everest (8,000m) has, we are told, "become a junk yard filled with hundreds of empty oxygen bottles, food tins, tent poles, butane gas cylinders and garbage". This sort of pollution threatens the natural beauty of the Himalayas, which is the very thing that people come to the mountains to enjoy. There is also the point that many of those who live in the

The Hunza Valley, photographed during the International Karakoram Project.

mountains regard the great peaks as gods; so the polluters blaspheme as well as desecrate. An even greater hazard threatens the north-facing slopes of the mountains. For here Soviet engineers are harnessing the waters of the Amu-Daria for irrigation; this has dried up the desert wells, and this in turn is threatening the traditional way of life of the desert people over a vast area. To the south of the mountains is another threat: deforestation, which is laying bare huge areas of what was once fertile countryside. And in the very heart of the mountains, in Tibet, the destruction of the monasteries has robbed a whole nation of its spiritual and cultural heritage.

We in the outside world have brought these problems to the Himalayas. We must not therefore wash our hands of them, and pretend they don't concern us. "No man," wrote John Donne, "is an Iland, intire of it selfe." So the well that is dying in the desert, the tree that is being felled in the foothills, the bell that is tolling for the desecrated monasteries, they are dying, falling, tolling not for some far-distant people but for you and me.

Index

Suggestions for Further Reading

Acknowledgements

Allen, Charles *A Mountain in Tibet,* 1982

Blunt, Wilfrid *The Golden Road to Samarkand,* 1973

Cameron, Ian *Mountains of the Gods,* 1984

Fleming, Peter *Bayonets to Lhasa,* 1961

Harrer, Heinrich *Seven Years in Tibet,* 1953

Herzog, Maurice *Annapurna,* 1952

Hillary, Edmund *High Adventure,* 1955

Hopkirk, Peter *Foreign Devils on the Silk Road,* 1980 and *Trespassers on the Roof of the World,* 1982

Keay, John *When Men and Mountains Meet,* 1977 and *The Gilgit Game,* 1979

Keenlyside, Francis *Peaks and Pioneers,* 1976

MacGregor, John *Tibet: A Chronicle of Exploration,* 1970

Mason, Kenneth *Abode of Snow,* 1955

Rowell, Galen *Mountains of the Middle Kingdom,* 1984

Shipton, Eric *That Untravelled World,* 1969

Unsworth, Walt *Everest,* 1981

Woodcock, George *Into Tibet: the Early British Explorers,* 1971

Illustrations which appear in this book are from the following sources:

Sayed Shah; page 35.
Pradip Rana; pages 24, 27.
Nazir Sabir; pages 37, 43, 51.
Marcel Ishac – Jonathan Cape Ltd. page 44.
Nigel de N. Winser/RGS International Karakoram Project; page 56.

All other illustrations are drawn from the Royal Geographical Society's library and archives. Those appearing on pages 9, 11–14, 16, 18, 21, 23, 25, 27, 30, 32, 33, 37 (bottom), 40–42 and 55 (bottom) were specially reproduced by Robert Glen.

Much material in 'Exploring the Himalayas' is derived from the author's previous book *Mountains of the Gods* published by Century Publishing Co. Ltd. The author acknowledges with many thanks his indebtedness to Century for permission to reproduce this material.

LONGMAN GROUP LIMITED
Longman House
Burnt Mill, Harlow, Essex CM20 2JE, England
and Associated Companies throughout the World

This book was co-ordinated by Michael Nyman and produced by Pamino Publications, 58/60 Kensington Church St., London W8.

Text © Donald Payne 1985

This edition © Pamino Publications 1985

First published 1985
ISBN 0 582 39286 1

Cameron, Ian, *1924–*
    Exploring the Himalayas. ——(Royal Geographical Society exploring series)
    1. Himalayas——Discovery and exploration
    Rn: Donald Gordon Payne I. Title II. Series
    915.4'04   DS485.H6

    ISBN 0–582–39286–1

Designed by Jim Reader
Production services by Book Production Consultants, Cambridge

Printed in Great Britain by Blantyre Printing & Binding Co. Ltd., Glasgow